A GUIDE TO THE SAINTS OF WALES AND THE WEST COUNTRY

A GUIDE
to
THE SAINTS
of
WALES
and the
WEST COUNTRY

by
RAY SPENCER

Copyright © Ray Spencer 1991.
Published by
LLANERCH ENTERPRISES.
ISBN 0947992 57 X.

PREFACE

When people think about 'saints' most will immediately think of Christ's apostles (the twelve disciples) or maybe St Francis of Assisi, that well known thirteenth-century man of God and mystic, known not just to Roman Catholics but to every child of school-age.

However, in the south-west of England and in Wales when you mention the 'saints' most people will be able to think of St David or perhaps St Petroc, though they may not know just who they were nor when they lived.

Wales and the south-west of England abound with the names of saints, many long ago lost in the realms of the so-called Dark Ages. But who were these people? St David patron saint of Wales died around 589 A.D., and was in those days of the Celtic Church, archbishop of Menevia and the founder of that famous monastery of Glyn Rhosyn (St David's) in west Wales. St Petroc also a Welshman is said to have gone to Rome and met the pope; he too was the founder of monasteries and churches, mainly in Devon and Cornwall; indeed Padstow, formerly Pertocstow, is named after him.

Many myths and legends have been attributed to these saints of the old Celtic Church, though I must stress that they are legends rather than history, for the 'Lives' of many of these saints were written centuries after their death, often embellished to suit the aims of their mediaeval biographers. Folklore has also also come down to us in stories written about their lives.

In this book I have delved into the lives, albeit briefly, of the saints of Wales and south-west England from Roman times until the Norman period. In fact, after the Romans departed, the next historical era in Wales and the South West was the Age of Saints of the Celtic Church. Many of these saints owe their beginnings to St Patrick a Romano-British saint of the fifth century. He converted much of Ireland, including the nobility to the Christian faith, and some of them became ardent evangelists.

The influence of these Celtic missionaries, contemporaries of SS Patrick and David, soon spread far and wide through Wales, south-west England, and into Brittany, in what nowadays we might refer to as the 'Celtic fringe.'

They built monasteries and churches and set up Celtic crosses; holy wells too were associated with them, though many had pre-Christian pagan origins. The saints often made good use of these wells; often the legends of the saints mention springs bursting forth on the sites of martyrdoms. These wells have been associated with folklore down the centuries.

Many place-names in Wales and the South West owe their origin to the Age of the Saints; thus in Welsh the word 'Llan' means an enclosure or church, and it is often followed by the name of a Saint; for example, Llandewi, the Church of St David, Llangybi the Church of St Cybi, etc. The saints' churches, with their Celtic crosses and holy wells became places of pilgrimage, with the relics of a particular saint being venerated and their shrines the site of cures and miracles.

This book gives a brief biography of these saints who were men and women of great sanctity, vision and strength. I have included three maps showing the monastic sites and places associated with the early saints of Wales, Cornwall, and the rest of south-west England. With these maps are lists of some of the less well-known saints. Information is given also concerning dates, places of veneration, and feast days - where possible, although I must add that very little is known about some of the early saints.

The majority of saints in this book are honoured by the Church in Wales, and the Anglican Church in south-west England, and also by the Orthodox Church in Britain; some are venerated by the Roman Catholic Church, including SS David, Non, Petroc, Tudwal and Winefride. St David patron saint of Wales is the only one thought to have been canonized (in 1120) though this is uncertain; his cultus was allowed by Pope Callistus II in the same year, however.

For certain the saints have left their mark on the beautiful countryside of Wales and south-west England, with their ancient churches, holy wells and crosses standing as a reminder of those men and women of long ago.

Finally, I might add that this book does not pretend to be an accurate portrayal of history, but to introduce the reader to the saints as they are known from their legends; the reader must remember throughout that much of what I have written is 'according to the legend'.

Ray Spencer, Nelson, 1990.

CONTENTS

Preface	5
1. The Saints of Wales:	11
Afan, Almedha, Aneurin, Armael, Asaph	12
Athan, Austoll, Barry	13
Beuno, Briavel, Bridgit	15
Brioc, Brychan, Brynach	16
Budock, Cadfan	17
Cadfarch, Cadoc	18
Cadwaladr, Callwen, Canna	19
Caradoc, Carannog	20
Ceitho, Celynen & companions, Cenydd	21
Cewydd, Clether	23
Clodock	24
Collen, Colman, Crallo	25
Cungar, Curig	26
Cwyfan, Cybi	27
Cynfarch, Cynllo, David	29
Decuman	31
Deiniol, Deiniol Fab, Derfel Gadarn	32
Dingat, Dogmael	33
Domnoc, Dubricius	34
Dwynwen	35
Eilian, Elvis	36
Endelienta, Ernin, Finan, Garmon	37
Gildas 39	
Glywys 40	
Govan 41	
Govan, Gwen, Gwendoline, Gwenfyl	42
Gwladys, Gwynllyw	43
Gwynnog, Helen of Caernarfon	44
Henwyn, Illtud	46
Illudiana	47
Ishmael, Julius & Aaron	48
Justinian	49
Kentigern	50
Keyne	51

Kywere, Leonorius, Llawdog, Llechid	52
Llibio, Llily, Llionio, Lluwchaiarn, Llyr, Llud	53
Mabyn, Madern, Madoc	54
Madrun 55	55
Maglorius, Malo	56
Mawgan, Melangell	58
Mellon, Menefrida	60
Meriadoc, Merrin, Mewan	61
Morwenna, Nectan	62
Nennoca	63
Non	64
Oudoceus	66
Pabo, Padarn	67
Paulinus	68
Petroc	69
Sadwrn	70
Samson	71
Seiriol	73
Sulien, Teilo	74
Tewdric	76
Trillo, Tudno, Tudwal	77
Tudy	78
Tydfil, Tysilio	79
Winefride	81
Winnoc	83
2. Some Other Saints of Wales:	84
Aelearn, Baglan, Beulan, Bilo, Bodfan, Caffo, Caron, Cawdraf, Ceidio, Ceinwr, Cian, Cyfyw, Cynfelin, Cynog, Dunawd	84
Dwywe, Dyfan, Edeyrn, Edie, Einion, Elerius, Ellyw, Eurgain, Ffili, Ffwyst, Gasteynin, Geinwen, Gover, Gredfyn	85
Gredifael, Gristolus, Gwaur, Gwenfaen, Gwerfyl, Gwyddfarch, Gwyndaf, Gwynno, Idloes, Iestyn, Igon, Ina, Ishan, Ishow, Keneder,	86
Llawen, Llewellyn, Maches, Macmoil, Mael, Maelog, Maethlu, Marcella, Meugan, Padrig, Peblig, Pedoric, Peris, Pyro	87

Rhwydrys, Rhychwyn, Rhydian, Rhystud, Sannan,
Saran, Saturnin, Sawel, Tecwyn, Tegai, Tegfedd,
Tegla, Trithyd, Tudur, Tunabius, Twrog   88
Tybie, Tyfodwg, Weonard, Wrw, Wyddelan   90
Map No 1 Wales: The Monstic Sites associated
with the saints of Wales   91
Key to Map No 1 Wales   92-95
Map No 2 South-West England: the monastic sites
and places associated with the saints of Wales 96
Key to Map No 2 The South West   97-98
3. The Saints of South-West England: 99
Arilda, Athvenna, Boniface of Crediton, Breaca,
Breague, Breward, Buryan, Cerrian, Columba,
Congar   99
Constantine, Credan, Crewenna, Crida, Culbone,
Day, Dominica, Enoder, Enodoc, Erme, Erth,
Euny   100
Eval, Genny, Geraint, Germoe, Gonand, Gorran,
Gulval, Gwennapa, Gwinear, Gwithian, Hydroc,
Ia, Illogan   101
Indract, Ive, Judware, Just, Kea, Ladoca, Levan,
Lide, Lidgean, Madron, Manaca, Manaccus,
Mawes   102
Mawnan, Meubred, Mylor, Neot, Newlyn, Piala,
Pinnock, Piran, Rayne, Ruan   105
Selyf, Sennaira, Sennanae, Sidwell, Sithney,
Stediana, Symphorian, Teath, Torney, Urith,
Veep, Wendron   106
Wethenoc, Whyte, Winwaloe, Wulfric, Wyllow 108
Map No 3 South-West England: The Monastic Sites
and Places associated with the Saints   109
Key to Map No 3 South-West England   110-111
Bibliography   112

ST ARTHMAEL
from stained glass at S Sauveur, Dinan.

1. The Saints of Wales.

ST AFAN, or Avan, died 6c, Bishop, 16th November. He was the cousin of St. David and the founder of a church at Llanafan Fawr in Powys; the church of Llanafan near Aberystwyth also bears his name. Very little is known about him, though a tombstone which may be his can still be seen at Llanafan Fawr.

ST ALMEDHA, Aled, Eiluned, or Elwedda, died 6c, Virgin and Martyr, 1st August. A daughter of king Brychan Brycheiniog. She founded the first church at Llanelwedd, which is near to Builth Wells in Powys. Apparently Almedha later suffered a martyr's death, and miracles occurred at her shrine soon after.

ST ANEURIN (Anierin Gwawdrydd), died 7c, Monk, 26th October. Born in southern Scotland but educated at Llancarfan in south Glamorgan. He became a monk and was famous for his seventh century poem 'Y Gododin' which described the famous battle of Cattraeth (603); the said battle took place in the North.

It seems quite likely that after Cattraeth he returned to Wales and possibly died at Llancarfan. Anierin Gwawdrydd is still considered to be one of the great bards of Wales.

ST ARMAEL, Arthmael, or Ermael, died 552, Abbot, 16th August. He was born in south Wales and was the cousin of SS Cadfan and Samson. Armael became a missionary in Brittany and built monasteries at Saint-Armel-des-Bochaux (Plouarmel), and Ploermel.

ST ASAPH, Asaf, or Asa, died 601, Bishop, 1st May. He was very probably born in the Strathclyde region of Scotland, but he and his family migrated to North Wales where Asaph became a monk. Then later he met St Kentigern (Cyndeyrn in Welsh) who had been banished from his bishopric of Glasgow in Scotland, and under his direction Asaph founded the monastery of Llanelwy in 550 AD, renamed St Asaph in the twelfth century.

A cathedral now stands on the site of the Celtic monastery. It could be that Asaph later became the first bishop of Llanelwy, although this is thought somewhat unlikely. Asaph also founded a monastery at Llanasa in Clwyd and his holy well (Ffynnon Asa) can be found in the nearby village of Cwm. Some famous legends and miracles have been attributed to him down the centuries.

ST ATHAN, Tathai, or Tathaneus, died 524, Abbot and Bishop, 26th December. He was born in Ireland and was the son of king Tathalius. It seems he decided to leave his father's court in order to become a missionary, and he came to Wales in the late fifth century, landing at Portskewett in Gwent. Then Athan founded a monastery at Llandathan (St Athan) in south Glamorgan, but in the year 500 AD he built his most famous monastic school at Caerwent and taught many Welsh saints. He has sometimes been referred to as bishop of Caerwent, but it is unlikely that he ever was a bishop. St Athan was renowned as a miracle-worker.

ST AUSTOLL, or Austell, died 6c, Abbot, 28th June. A Welsh monk and disciple of St Samson, who was his godfather. Austoll accompanied SS Mewan and Samson to Cornwall and founded the church of St Austell near Bodmin. Later he became a missionary in Brittany. He died at St Meen, near Rennes, and was buried there.

ST BARRY, Barric, or Barruc, died 6c, Hermit, 27th September. An Irish monk who journeyed to S. Wales and became a disciple of St Cadoc. He built a church at what is now Barry Island in

ST BRIDGET
after Cahier.

South Glamorgan. The ruins of his church overlook the harbour entrance. St Barruc's holy well was once visited for the cure of headaches.

ST BEUNO, died 640, Abbot, 21st April. He was born at Berriew in Powys or possibly in Herefordshire, the son of Hywgi ap Gwynllyw, and educated by St Tangusius at Caerwent. Beuno later became a missionary and founded monasteries at Llanveynoe (Llanfeuno) in Herefordshire, and at Berriew and Llanymynech in northern Powys.

Traditionally he restored to life his niece St Winefride at Treffynnon (Holywell) in Clwyd. In 616 AD he built his famous monastery at Clynnog Fawr on the Lleyn Peninsula, and died there in 640 AD. His holy well at Clynnog was renowned for its healing properties; another St Beuno's well can be found at Tremeirchion in Cwyd.

Apart from Clynnog Fawr, he has other church dedications at Trefdraeth and Aberffraw in Anglesey, at Pistyll near Nefyn in Gwynedd, Whitford in Clwyd, Berriew and Guilsfield in Powys.

ST BRIAVEL, died 6c? Hermit, 17th June. Very little is known about St Briavel, though it seems probable that he was a Celtic hermit who founded the first church at the place today called St Briavels in Gloucestershire, although the present church is dedicated to St. Mary. Briavel could be the Welsh St Briamel or even Brioc?

ST BRIDGET, Bridgit, Bride, or Ffraid, died 525, Abbess, 1st (or 3rd) February. Ffraid in Welsh is actually Bride - Bridget, that is St Bridget. She was born at Faughart in Ireland and was famous for founding the renowned monastery of Kildare (490). A number of places in Wales are named after her, such as Llansantffraid and St Brides in Dyfed, and also St Brides Major in S. Glamorgan. She has other dedications in Anglesey, Gwynedd, Powys, and at Skenfrith in Gwent. This all points towards the close ties between the early Celtic churches of both Wales and Ireland.

ST BRIOC, Briocus, or Brieuc, died 510, Abbot, 1st May. He was born near Cardigan, possibly at Llandyfriog, where he founded a monastery. He went into Cornwall later, and St Breock near Padstow bears his name. In 490 AD Brioc settled in Brittany and built two more monasteries, one near Treguier and the other at what is today St Brieuc, though the bishopric was established much later than the saint. Legend says he lived to be over a hundred, and his kindness brought him many followers.

ST BRYCHAN, or Brechan, died 5c. King, 6th April. Brychan king of Brecknock (Brycheiniog) or today Brecon, was the son of King Anlach of Ireland and Marchell, but his family came over to Wales in the fifth century. He is said to have been a saintly king who ruled his kingdom fairly well, though at all times with a firm yet steady hand.

But Brychan is mostly remembered through the lives of his children; the exact number varies between twenty and sixty, with thirty-six being most likely, twenty five of whom were daughters. A stone at Llanspyddid church near Brecon may mark his burial place, but he probably died on the Isle of Anglesey.

ST BRYNACH, or Brenach, died 570, Abbot, 7th April. An Irish nobleman who after being converted to Christianity came to south-west Wales and married the daughter of a chieftain, but she tried in vain to subdue his religious fervour. He founded churches along the Gwaun Valley in Dyfed - at Henry's Moat (Castell-Hendre), Pontfaen and Cwm-yr-Eglwys (now a ruin).

In 540 AD Brynach founded a monastery at Nevern and from time to time he would climb to the top of nearby Carn Ingli in order to speak to the angels. Beside St Brynach's church in Nevern is a tenth-century Celtic cross upon which the first cuckoo of the spring sings on the saint's day (7th April). Also in the village is a pilgrim's cross which is carved upon a rock face. St Brynach has other church dedications in Dyfed, Powys and S. Glamorgan.

After returning from a long pilgrimage to Rome he settled at Braunton in Devon, and here suckling pigs showed him where to build his church. Braunton people refer to him as St Brannoc.

ST BUDOCK, Buddoc, or Beuzec, died 585, Bishop, 9th December. Born in either south-west Wales or Ireland. A church was once named after him near Steynton in Dyfed. He evangelized mainly in Devon and Cornwall where he has a few church dedications.

In 570 AD Budock became a hermit at Brehat in Brittany and founded a monastery on the isle of Laurea. He was consecrated bishop of Dol in 575. The relics of St Budock are at Plourin.

ST CADFAN, or Cadmanus, died 540, Abbot, 1st November. There are two conflicting lives of St Cadfan, but the one generally accepted is this: Cadfan was a prince of Brittany and the son of Eneos Lydewig and St Gwen Teibrian. In the early part of the sixth century he was deposed by the Franks, so he decided to renounce his royal title. Later, Cadfan set out for Cornwall, and then Wales, with some other disciples - SS Cynllo, Mael, Padarn, Sulien and Tydecho.

In 516 AD he settled at Tywyn in Gwynedd and built a monastery, and was the founder of the first church at Llangadfan in Powys. His holy well in Tywyn churchyard was once famous because the water was used to cure rheumatism; an inscribed stone in the church could be the saint's burial stone.

King Einion asked Cadfan to help him build a monastery on Bardsey Island and he elected Cadfan as first abbot. Nothing remains of the Celtic monastery now, and there are only the ruins of a much later Augustinian Abbey. St Cadfan probably died on Bardsey Island where, according to legend, another twenty-thousand saints are also buried. This saint is also venerated in Brittany, especially in Finisterre and in the Cotes-du-Nord region.

ST CADFARCH, died 6c, Confessor, 24th Oct. The son of Caradoc Freichfras, and founder of a church at Penegoes near Machynlleth in Powys. The village of Penegoes is famous for its health wells.

ST CADOC, Cadocus, or Cattwg, died 560, Abbot, 25th September. Born either at Bochriwcarn (Fochriw) in mid Glamorgan, or at Allt-Gwynlliw in Newport, Gwent. He was the son of St. Gwynlliw king of Gwent and St Gwladys daughter of King Brychan. In 500 AD Cadoc went to be educated at Llanilltud-Fawr, and later by St Tathan at Caerwent. It seems he founded his first church in Caerleon, though his principal monastery was at Llancarfan in South Glamorgan, and this became a major centre of learning.

He founded numerous churches; there are two Llangadogs in Dyfed, Llangattock in Powys, Cadoxton in West Glamorgan; also Llangattock Lingoed, Llangattock-Vibon-Avel, Llangattock-Nigh-Usk, Penrhos, Raglan, Clytha, Trevethin and Monmouth, in Gwent.

Cadoc went over to Ireland with St Gildas and, possibly, St David. He returned to Wales for a short period, then, in 546 AD, he journeyed to Brittany and became a hermit near Etel. Legend says that he became bishop of Benevento in Italy and was martyred there, but it is more likely that he died at Llancarfan in Wales when his monastery was attacked by pagans. Some scholars suggest that he even died at Benevium (Weedon) in Northamptonshire. St Cadoc was the cousin of King Arthur and was one of the two knights who were apparently put in charge of the legendary holy grail.

An ancient stone discovered at Llandefaelog-Fach in Powys, and now in the church, is perhaps Cadoc's burial stone. He wrote the famous "Wisdom of Cattwg" - or Cattwg Doeth.

ST CADWALADR, died 664, King and Confessor, 12th November. He was king of Gwynedd (North Wales), and the son of King Cadwallon. It is known that he was a peaceful man who was very kind to his people, though he did go into battle against King Edwin of Northumbria (633), and against Wessex (658) at Peonne in Somerset. Cadwaladr founded the church of Llangadwaladr on the island of Anglesey, and Llangadwaladr in Clwyd. He also has a church dedicated to him just east of Newport in Gwent.

This saint is depicted wearing royal attire, and holding his sceptre and orb, in a stained-glass window at Llangadwaladr church, Anglesey.

ST CALLWEN, died 5c, Virgin, 1st November. She was a daughter of King Brychan Brycheiniog and sister of St Gwenfyl. Little is known about her, though she has church dedications at Callwen near Ystradgynlais in Powys, and at Cellan in Dyfed.

ST CANNA, died 6c., 25th October. She was the daughter of Tewdr Mawr and wife of St Sadwrn, but it is not known where she came from, though she, her husband, and son St Crallo may have come from Brittany. St Canna has church dedications at Llangan in South Glamorgan, and also at Llangan in Dyfed.

A Celtic cross with carvings upon it can still be seen in Llangan churchyard, South Glamorgan. As for St Canna, she went with St Sadwrn to Anglesey and her name is mentioned on a tombstone in Llansadwrn church. Her holy well at Llangan in Dyfed was visited by pilgrims for the cure of intestinal complaints.

ST CARADOC, died 1124, Priest, 14th April. He was born at Brecon in Powys. As a young man he was employed as a musician at the court of Rhys ap Tewdwr, prince of South Wales, but he later angered the prince when he lost two prize dogs. Now that he was greatly disliked by the prince, Caradoc became a pilgrim and journeyed as far as Llandaff where he was tonsured as a monk.

Shortly afterwards he settled as a hermit on Barry Island in South Glamorgan, and later at St Cenydd's church at Llangenydd on the Gower Peninsula. Caradoc then went to live on a small island near the Pembroke coast, but the island was raided by the Normans and others; so he moved to Haroldston (St Isell's) and died there in the year 1124. His saintly body was later buried in St David's cathedral, where his shrine can still be seen, and at which, long ago, miracles were reported. A holy well is named after him at Haverfordwest, and a church is dedicated to St Caradoc at Lawrenny north-west of Pembroke.

ST CARANNOG, Carantoc, or Carantocus, died 6c, Abbot, 16th May. He was born in the Cardigan area and was the son of Carwn ap Ceredig (who was related to Cunedda Wledig). It seems that in his youth he went to Ireland and was educated there, and after returning to Wales he founded a monastery at Llangrannog in Dyfed.

Then Carannog decided to take the gospel to other lands, though he was uncertain just where to start.

He cast a portable stone altar into the Bristol Channel vowing to build a church wherever it landed. However he lost all sight of the altar on the way. Later, King Arthur found the altar-stone, and he thought it would make an excellent table, though everything he put on top just slid right off. When St Carannog arrived on the scene he convinced Arthur of his holiness by ridding the area of a huge serpent which even the king's knights couldn't destroy. Arthur was so impressed that he returned the altar-stone to the saint and gave him some land for a church.

Carannog first met King Arthur at a place called Dindraetho (Dunster) in Somerset, and went on to found a monastery at nearby Carhampton. Crantock in Cornwall is also named after him, and here he built another church. A holy well in the village of Crantock was visited by locals for the cure of worms in the body. In Brittany both Carantec and St Caradec bear his name.

SS CEITHO, CELYNEN, GWYN, GWYNARO and GWYNOG, died 6c, 29th June. The church of Pumpsaint near Lampeter in Dyfed commemorates five saintly brothers of the family of Cunedda. According to legend, they are sleeping in a nearby cave awaiting a certain holy bishop; only then will they awake to continue their mission.

A stone close to the Roman mines at Pumpsaint bears the foot-marks of these saints, though sceptics might disagree with this. At one time, five healing wells existed at nearby Cwm Cerwyni. The village of Llanpumsaint near Carmarthen is also associated with the five saints, as are other churches in Dyfed and Gwynedd.

ST CENYDD, Kyned, Kynedus, or Kenneth, died

ST CENYDD
from statue at Ploumelin.

587, Abbot, 1st August. He was the son of Prince Diochocus of Brittany whose family migrated to Wales, and settled on the Gower. Cenydd, however, was born deformed and was cast out by the prince, but according to legend King Arthur granted the child clemency.

Then the child was placed in a basket on the river Loughor near Llanelli, and the tide carried the basket out to sea. But miraculously some gulls came to the river and carried the basket to Worm's Head where baby Cenydd was suckled by a deer. After a while the baby was found by St Gildas and he brought up the child and taught him about the Christian faith. Cenydd was educated by SS Illtud and Cadoc, but he wished to seek a more solitary life; so he became a hermit on Burry Holms, and was visited by St David. He founded a monastery at Llangennith on the Gower Peninsula, and taught many local hermits. Two more churches besides Llangennith are dedicated to him; they are at Llangennech in Dyfed, and Senghenydd in Mid Glamorgan.

In 544 AD Cenydd became a missionary in Brittany, and later founded a church at Ploumelin, where he died around 587 AD.

ST CEWYDD, died 6c, Hermit, 15th July. He was probably one of the sons of King Brychan, and became a hermit in a cave at Aberedw near Builth Wells in Powys (his cave was situated in the Aberedw Rocks). This saint may also have founded the first church in the village. A church is dedicated to St Cewydd at Disserth near Llandrindod Wells. It seems likely that he became a disciple of St Cadoc in South Glamorgan, and he may be the same saint that is venerated at Llangynwyd near Maesteg.

ST CLETHER, Clechre, Cleer, Clear, or Clarus, died 550, Hermit, 4th November. Born near

Carmarthen the son of King Cledwin or Clydwyn. As a young man he was given some land at Nevern in Dyfed, and he lived at a fortification called Castell-Nevern, now an over-grown mound behind Nevern church. Here Clether was converted to Christianity by St Brynach. The town of St Clears near Carmarthen, despite its name, is not connected with this saint.

When his territories were invaded by Dyfnwal, a pagan chieftain, Clether fled to Cornwall and became a hermit in the Inny Valley. He founded the church of St Clether, near Camelford. The saint's holy well stands just west of the church and below a rocky cliff. The well, which was famous for its healing properties, stands beside a small chapel. Another church and holy well are dedicated to him at St Cleer near Bodmin, and yet another well is named after him at Philham near Hartland in Devon; this was a healing well, and it retains an image of the saint.

ST CLODOCK, Clydog, or Clydawg, died 520, King and Martyr, 3rd November. He was born in Ewyas (south-west Herefordshire) son of King Gwynnar, and a grandson of King Brychan. Upon the death of his father, Clodock became king of Ewyas, an area which includes part of Herefordshire and what used to be Monmouthshire. He was very pious, peace-loving, and always kind and charitable to his people. Later, a nobleman's daughter fell in love with him, and they were soon married; however, not long after, while out hunting, King Clodock was brutally killed by a jealous enemy who also wanted to marry Clodock's new wife.

The king's body was placed on a cart pulled by two oxen, but the two animals refused to go on and the chains all broke. The people took this to be a sign from God, and buried their king near the river Monnow. Soon afterwards they decided to build a church to enshrine King Clodock's holy body, and a shrine was erected in his memory. The place was later referred to as Merthyr-Clitauc (or today, Clodock) in Herefordshire. And long ago, miracles occurred at his shrine inside Clodock church.

ST COLLEN, died 6c, Hermit, 21st May. He was probably born in mid Wales a descendant of Prince Caradoc Freichfras, and one of his brothers was called St Maethlu (of Llanfaethlu) on the isle of Anglesey. According to legend, Collen was a knight of King Arthur, and went to Rome where of all things he slew a pagan knight in front of the pope. Then he settled in Brittany and built a church at Llangoelan in Finistere.

Collen eventually became a hermit (perhaps abbot) at Glastonbury in Somerset; however, he longed for greater solitude and was soon back in Wales. He lived as a hermit in the Vale of Llangollen, in a cave by the river Dee, and he built his church close-by. The town of Llangollen in Clwyd bears his name and the present St Collen's church marks the site of the saint's early foundation. Apparently St Collen was a man of miracles; he once sprinkled holy water on a fairy king, who then vanished into thin air, and he rid the Llangollen area of a terrifying giantess. St Collen is patron saint of Llangollen in Clwyd, and he has another church dedication at Colan in Cornwall.

ST COLMAN, died 610, Bishop, 7th June (20th November in Wales). The churches of Llangolman and Capel Colman in Dyfed are said to be dedicated to St Colman, abbot and first bishop of Dromore in County Down. He died at Arboe beside Lough Neagh in Ireland.

ST CRALLO, died 6c, Monk, 25th October. Very little if anything is known about him except that he was the son of SS Sadwrn and Canna. He probably founded the first church at Coychurch in Mid Glamorgan, where there is a very fine Celtic cross inside the church of St Crallo, which may mark the saint's burial place.

ST CUNGAR, Cyngar, Congar, or Dochau, died 520, Abbot, 27th November. He was probably born at Llanwngar near St David's in Dyfed, son of St Geraint and uncle of St Cybi; his brother was St Selyf of Cornwall and two of his cousins were King Arthur and St Illtud. Cungar became a missionary in Devon and also founded monasteries at Congresbury and Banwell in Somerset. When the Saxons overran Somerset, Cungar fled to Cornwall and stayed with his sister St Kywere, and built a monastery at St Kew.

Then later he returned to Wales and became a disciple of his nephew St Cybi. At Llandough near Cardiff he established another monastic foundation; the other Llandough near Cowbridge also has a church dedication to him. He and his nephew Cybi went over to Ireland and stayed on the island of Aran with St Enda, but after four years they came back to Wales. Cungar settled at Ynys Gyngar near Criccieth in Gwynedd and built the church of Llangefni in Anglesey; the church at Hope in Clwyd may be dedicated to him, though there was another St Cungar (Congar) who was a disciple of St Cadoc; he built the church of Lanivet in Cornwall, and others in Brittany; his feast-day is 13th February.

ST CURIG or Cyric, died 550, Abbot and Bishop, 17th February or 16th June. An Irish missionary who had been a soldier in his youth, but on his conversion to Christianity his life changed. He set sail for Wales and landed in Cardigan Bay; first settling at Eisteddfa Gurig and later Llangurig, in Powys. Here the saint was given some land by King Maelgwn Gwynedd, and he built a monastery on it. St Curig has sometimes been called a bishop, but this is somewhat uncertain, although he probably did attend the synod at Llanddewi Brefi. One other notable church dedication to him is Capel-Curig in Gwynedd, and a few other places in Gwynedd and Dyfed might perhaps be associated with him.

ST CWYFAN, died 7c, Confessor, 7th June. He was probably a monk and disciple of St Beuno, whom he accompanied to North Wales in the early seventh century. A church or monastery was founded by him at Llangwyfan near Denbigh in Clwyd, and also at Llangwyfan in Anglesey. St Cwyfan's stone (Maen Achwyfan) which dates from 1000 AD is located one mile west of Whitford in Clwyd. But this ancient stone is an eleven foot high Celtic wheel-cross covered in carved patterns; St Cwyfan may have preached on this site. The church at Dyserth in Clwyd is dedicated to SS Cwyfan and Bridget.

ST CYBI, Cuby, Kebi or Kebius, died 555, Abbot, 8th November. He was born in Cornwall, son of St Selyf and St Gwen (sister of St Non). After receiving a good education, young Cybi went on a pilgrimage to Rome and the Holy Land. On his return he founded monasteries at Duloe and Tregony in Cornwall, and churches at Cubert (where he has a famous holy well) and also Landulph.

Cybi set out for South Wales with his uncle St Cungar and SS Feulan, Maelog and Llibio, who have church dedications in both Anglesey and Powys. Cybi built a monastery at Llangybi (Llangibby-on-Usk) in Gwent, and on the way to see St David he built yet another church at Llangybi near Lampeter. After visiting Ireland he came to North Wales and settled on the Lleyn peninsula

ST DAVID
after Baring Gould & Fisher.

where another church and holy well near Pwllheli bear his name.

In 540 AD he built his famous monastery at Caer-Gybi (Holyhead) in Anglesey, in the ruins of a Roman fort and upon land given to him by Maelgwn Gwynedd. St Cybi died there in 555 AD and was apparently buried on Bardsey Island.

ST CYNFARCH or Kinemark, died 6c, Confessor, 8th September. A disciple of St Dubricius who founded the church of St Kinemark (Llangynfarch) in Gwent. And another saint of this name was venerated at Llanfair-Dyffryn near Ruthin in Clwyd.

ST CYNLLO, died 560, Confessor, 17th July. He was either a native of Wales or of Brittany, and was also a missionary with SS Cadfan, Padarn and Tydecho. He probably founded churches at Llangunllo and Llanbister in Powys, and at Llangynlo in Dyfed.

ST DAVID (Dewi Sant), died 589 or 601, Archbishop, 1st March. He was born around the year 500 AD in somewhat miraculous circumstances at Caerfai in Dyfed. According to legend, St Non, his mother, gave birth to him during a thunderstorm, whilst at the same time being pursued by King Sant (of Cardigan) and his warriors. St Non's holy well and chapel, one mile south of St David's (Ty Dewi) mark the birthplace of the patron saint of Wales. Shortly afterwards, baby David was baptized at nearby Porth-Clais by St Elvis (Eilbyn) bishop of Emlech in Ireland.

David was brought up at Henfynyw near Aberaeron in Dyfed, and then became a monk at Ty Gwyn under St Paulinus, who taught and educated him. Both Paulinus and David retired to an island of the west Wales coast in order to seek solitude; here an angel instructed Paulinus to let David go out into the world.

David, now a priest, visited many monastic centres in Wales, England, and perhaps Ireland, making his own foundations at Glascwm, Llangyfelach and Raglan in Wales; also churches at Glastonbury in Somerset, Leominster in Herefordshire. David inherited from his father, Sant, a monastery at Henllan to the east of Cardigan, and he became abbot there for a short period. But he was commanded by an angel to go to a place called Glyn Rhosyn (now St David's) - Ty Dewi). It was here in the year 530 AD that he founded his most famous monastery.

Many disciples gathered around him, they included: SS Aedhan (Madoc), Ishmael, Padarn and Teilo. Here David and his monks led a very austere and spartan life. Work was carried out in silence, no animals were used on the land - the monks doing the work themselves; no meat was eaten, nor any wine drank, though water was a necessity, and this led to David being referred to as 'David the Water Drinker' (Dewi Ddyfrwr).

He and his followers preached the gospel throughout Wales, Brittany, Devon and Cornwall; thus a large number of places especially in Wales (those called Llandewi or Capel Dewi) are named after him. Legend says David and three disciples travelled to Rome and Jerusalem where they were received by the patriarch, and were given gifts to take back with them to Wales.

David became famous for the leading role he played at the great synod of Llandewi Brefi, where legend says that the ground rose up under him in order that he could be seen and heard by everyone. He was also proclaimed archbishop of Menevia (Mynyw) and primate of all Wales.

St David died about the year 589 or 601 AD at Glyn Rhosyn, and was buried in the monastery church; his relics, with those of St Justinian his confessor, now lie in a casket near the high altar in St David's cathedral. His shrine is in the north choir-aisle. St David's canonization seems somewhat doubtful.

He figures very strongly in the lives of many kings, including Arthur, Cunedda, Ceredig and Brychan; he was, of course, related to them and also to SS Cadoc, Dubricius, Illtud and Sulien, among others. At least four holy wells bear his name; they are: Ffynnon Ddewi, south of Clegyr-Boia in Dyfed, Brawdy and Henfynyw in Dyfed, and Newton-Nottage in Mid-Glamorgan.

ST DECUMAN, Decumanus or Degyman, died 6c? Hermit and Martyr, 12th November. He was of Welsh birth but may have been educated in Ireland. It seems that he was a missionary in north Somerset, and settled as a hermit at Watchet near Dunster. Decuman began to convert the local people to Christianity, but one day while at prayer there, one or more pagan Saxons set upon the holy man and beheaded him, because they did not like what he was trying to do. The saint picked up his severed head and carried it for two hundred yards to a spring (now known as St Decuman's well); here he washed his head in the water. The saint's holy well is located on a hillside not very far from Watchet church. Another church at nearby St Decuman's also bears his name.

According to legend the saint carried his severed head back to Wales, sailing on a bundle of twigs; when he landed at Rhoscrowther (Llandegyman) in Dyfed, a second holy well burst forth from the ground where he rested his severed head. This second St Decuman's well is located just south of the church going towards Angle Bay. One other legend has St Decuman martyred in South Wales but on his arrival in Somerset he was restored to life at Watchet, only to suffer martydom again at a later date, which does make things rather confusing.

ST DEINIOL, or Daniel (the Elder), died 584, Bishop, 11th September. Born in Strathclyde, Scotland, of the family of Coel Godebog, king of the North Britons. Deiniol came to North Wales in the early sixth-century, and in the year 525 AD settled at Bangor Fawr on the Menai Straits where he received some land from King Cadwallon; thus he was able to build a church and monastery there. In 540 AD Deiniol refounded a monastery at Bangor-is-y-Coed (Bangor Iscoed) on the river Dee in Clwyd, and by about 550 AD his father St Dunwyd (Donat) had become abbot.

Deiniol attended the synod of Llandewi Brefi where he was consecrated Bishop of Bangor-Fawr by St David. On his way back to the north, he founded the church of Llandeiniol, near Aberystwyth in Dyfed, and he and his disciples built the churches of Llanfor and Llanuwchllyn near Lake Bala. Other dedications to Deiniol can be found at Marchwiail and Worthenbury in Clwyd, and also at Itton (Llandeiniol) in Gwent, and Llangarron in Herefordshire where he is called St Deinst. St Deiniol probably died at Bangor-Fawr, but he was buried on Bardsey Isle (Ynys Enlli). The cathedral at Bangor in Gwynedd is dedicated to St Deiniol.

ST DEINIOL FAB or Deiniol the Younger, died 6c, bishop, 23rd November. The son of St Deiniol of Bangor. He founded a church or monastery at Llandaniel-Fab in Anglesey, and a church at Llandeiniolen near Bangor in Gwynedd. [When his father died he succeeded him as bishop of Bangor].

ST DERFEL GADARN, died 560, Abbot, 6th April. He was probably a native of Wales, though some have suggested either Somerset or Cornwall. Derfel was a knight of King Arthur and in his youth he fought in the battle of Camlan (537). However, he decided to seek a life of seclusion, and became a hermit in Mid Wales - at Llandderfel in Gwynedd, where he founded a church.

It seems he was later called upon to become abbot of Bardsey, where he was eventually buried. At Llandderfel church are the remains of St Derfel's wooden horse, alas without the wooden image of the saint, which had moveable arms, legs and eyes. This image was taken to Smithfield in London in 1538 and burnt along with Blessed John Forest, who was a Franciscan friar and confessor to Catherine of Aragon. Friar Forest had refused to deny that the image had worked miracles; thus he was burnt with the image; the Welsh prophecy that the image would set a whole forest on fire came true.

Llandderfel church was once a place of pilgrimage, apparently anyone making an offering to the saint would be delivered out of hell. St Derfel's horse and staff remain inside the church.

ST DINGAT or Dengad, died 6c, Confessor, 1st November. He was the son of King Brychan Brycheiniog and was educated at Llancarfan by St Cadoc. Dingat founded the church at Dingestow (or Llandingat) in Gwent where he was perhaps a martyr, although this is uncertain, but he may have been buried there. He may have founded the church of Llandingat at Llandovery, in Dyfed. Another church at New Tredegar, Mid Glamorgan, bears his name.

ST DOGMAEL or Docmel, died 505, Abbot, 14th June. A Welsh monk who was the grandson of King Ceredig of Cardigan. After some monastic training in Ireland, he returned to Wales and settled in Anglesey - Llandogwel church is dedicated to him. St Dogmael later sailed down the Cardigan coast and founded a monastery just inland at what is today St Dogmaels (Llandudoch) in Dyfed; the ruined Tironesian abbey was built in 1115. St Thomas's church in the village possibly stands on the site of the Celtic monastery, and a fifth-century Celtic stone with the Ogham alphabet carved upon it can be found inside. St Dogmael probably founded the church of St Dogwell's in Dyfed, but it appears that he died in Brittany where he still has a fairly strong cultus.

ST DOMNOC, Dyfnog, or Modomnoc, died 6c, Abbot, 13th February. He was probably an Irish prince of the O'Neills, but he came to Wales and was educated by, and became the disciple of, St David. According to legend, he was a bee-keeper at St David's monastery of Glyn Rhosyn, and when he returned to Ireland the bees followed him across the sea. He eventually founded a monastery at Tibberaghny in County Kilkenny; some have claimed that he became bishop of Ossory in Ireland.

ST DUBRICIUS, Dyfrig, Devereux, died 546, Bishop, 4th or 14th November. Born around the year 460 AD at Madley in Herefordshire, son of princess Erbdil, she being the daughter of King Peibau of Erging (Archenfield), now part of Herefordshire. The birth of this famous churchman was miraculous. When Dubricius became a priest he built his first church at Madley, and soon afterwards a monastery at Ariconium (perhaps Weston-under-Penyard, near Ross-on-Wye). Other monasteries were built by him at Hentland some four miles west of Ross, and at Moccas near Bredwardine. He had a large following of disciples; they included SS Cynfarch, Pedoric (of Kilpeck), Samson and also Weonarth (of St Weonard's). With the help of St Samson he founded the monastery on Caldey Island, and then chose St Pyro as the first Abbot. Dubricius attended the famous synod of Llandewi-Brefi and consecrated St Samson bishop, though Dubricius himself resigned his own bishopric of Caerleon in favour of St David who then transferred the see to Mynyw; it is very unlikely, however, that Caerleon ever had a bishop; it could be that Dubricius was bishop of Llandaff. According to legend, St Dubricius crowned his nephew King Arthur at Caerleon in 518 AD.

In later life Dubricius retired to Bardsey Isle and died there. In 1120 his relics were brought to Llandaff cathedral. Churches are dedicated to him at Hentland, Ballingham, St Devereux, Whitchurch (and previously - Moccas and Llanwarne in Herefordshire), Gwenddwr in Powys, Llanrumney near Cardiff, Porlock in Somerset.

ST DWYNWEN, Dwynen, or Donwen, died 465, Virgin, 25th January. One of the daughters of King Brychan. She went with her father into North Wales and then became a hermitess on a small island in south-west Anglesey - Llanddwyn Island. Here Dwynwen founded a nunnery and church. The ruins of a sixteenth-century church mark the site of her nunnery. Legend says that prince Maelon fell in love with Dwynwen and wanted to marry her, though she rejected him. So she prayed to God and was granted three wishes, firstly that Maelon be unfrozen from a magic potion that she had given him, secondly that all her requests on behalf of lovers would be answered, and thirdly that she would never marry.

Her holy well and hermitage can still be seen at Llanddwyn; at one time the well had miraculous healing qualities, and the movement of fish foretold the destiny of anyone wishing to marry. People used to bring sick animals to be healed at her shrine in Llanddwyn church. St Dwynwen is patron saint of lovers.

ST EILIAN, Eilean, or Allan, died 543, Hermit, 12th or 14th January. According to legend he came from Rome, but it seems more likely that he was a native of Brittany or Cornwall. One day he overheard some people talking about Britain; they said that its people were not yet fully Christianized.

So Eilian returned home to tell his family and they all decided to go, and take the gospel to those far-off pagan lands. After a few weeks sailing he and his family reached Anglesey, and they settled first at Porth-yr-Ychan which is in the north-east of the island. Eilian founded a church close-by at the place now called Llaneilian, but this met with hostility from King Cadwallon; however an amicable agreement was reached later and Eilian healed the king of (spiritual) blindness.

He preached throughout Anglesey as far as Abergele on the mainland; a church is dedicated to him at Llaneilian-yn-Rhos in Clwyd. St Eilian's holy well (Ffynnon Eilian) is about half a mile north-east of Llaneilian church in Anglesey, though it is now dried-up; at one time pilgrims came to the well and visited a chapel which once stood on the site. It may be that St Eilian went later to Cornwall because there is a village called St Allen near Truro. Some have identified him with St Allan, bishop of Quimper in Brittany during the sixth century.

ST ELVIS, Ailbeus, Ailbhe, or Eilbyw, died 527, Bishop, 12th September. An Irish bishop of Emlech (Emily) County Tipperary. He came to Wales in the early sixth century and baptized the young St David at Porth-Clais in Dyfed. A church (now ruined) near Talbenny used to be dedicated to him, and an area to the south-east of Solva also bears the name of St Elvis.

ST ENDELIENTA or Endellion, died 5-6c, Virgin, 29th April. One of the many daughters of King Brychan who had a cultus in Cornwall. Endelienta founded the first church at St Endellion, and possibly became a nun at Tregony. According to legend, her cow was killed by a pagan landowner when it strayed onto his land. Two holy wells still bear her name at St Endellion in Cornwall.

ST ERNIN or Erninas, died 6c, Abbot, 2nd November. He was born in North Wales son of Helig ap Glannowg. Ernin became abbot of Bardsey Island (Ynis Enlli), but later went to Brittany and settled as a hermit, first at Duault, then at Locarn where his relics still lie inside the church which is dedicated to him.

ST FINAN, died 595, Confessor, 18th March. It is not known for certain where he was born; either North Wales, or maybe Scotland. He became a disciple of St Kentigern (Cyndeyrn) and founded the church of Llanffinnan in Anglesey. Then later when St Kentigern returned to Scotland Finan accompanied him and founded churches in the Aberdeen area, where he died in 595 AD.

ST GARMON, Garmonus, Germanus, or Harmon, died 480, Abbot and Bishop, 31st July. He was born in Brittany in 410 AD, though Ireland was often considered to have been his birthplace, and St Patrick his cousin. He may be identified with St Germanus of Auxerre, though Baring-Gould and Fisher considered him as a different saint.

In 440 AD Garmon travelled from Brittany to Ireland and stayed with St Patrick; then, ten years later, he came to West Wales and lived for a while in St Brioc's monastery near Cardigan.

ST GERMANUS
from stained glass, St Neot.

Then around the year 470 AD with the help of young St Illtud, he refounded a monastery at Llanilltud-Fawr (later Llantwit Major) in South Glamorgan, and Illtud eventually became its first abbot. Garmon returned to Brittany for a short time, but came back to Wales again, possibly also visiting St Patrick in Ireland.

He engaged a certain King Gwrtheyrn (Vortigern) in a series of magical fetes of strength on the Lleyn Peninsula, and also founded several churches in North Wales, including: Llanarmon and Capel-Garmon in Gwynedd, Llanarmon-yn-Ial and Llanarmon-dyffryn-Ceiriog in Clwyd. The church at St Harmon in Powys is also dedicated to him. That he was elected bishop on the Isle of Man seems quite probable, because the cathedral of St German on St Patrick's Isle is seemingly dedicated to him.

Long ago, pilgrims used to visit the saint's church at Llanarmon-yn-Ial in Clwyd, mainly because a statue of bishop Garmon was venerated there.

ST GILDAS (the Wise or Badonicus), died 570, Abbot, 29th January. He was born in lower Clydeside, Scotland, the son of Caw Cawlwyd, a chieftain of noble descent. His brothers were St Caffo (who was a martyr at Llangaffo in Anglesey) and St Maeliog (Maelog), who has church dedications at Llanfaelog in Anglesey, Llandefalle, Llandefaelog-tre-Graig, and Llowes in Powys. Inside Llowes church there is a seventh-century Celtic cross, sometimes referred to as St Maelog's cross.

Gildas was born around 497 AD, possibly as late as 516 AD. His surname Badonicus was apparently given to him because of a famous battle fought at the time of his birth, in which King Arthur won a great victory over the Saxons. As a boy (or perhaps an adult) Gildas came to Wales and was educated at Llanilltud Fawr in order to study literature and scripture. In 525 AD he is said to have accompanied St David to Ireland where he gained a wider knowledge of the monastic life. On returning to Wales he stayed with St Cadoc at Llancarfan, but shortly after went on a pilgrimage to Rome where he met the Pope.

In the year 537 AD Gildas settled on the tiny island of Flat Holm in the Bristol Channel; three years later, he wrote his famous work called 'De Excidio et Conquestu Britanniae' which tells of the decadence of the British clergy and secular kings.

Gildas went to Brittany in 544 AD and became a hermit on the island of Horat (Houat) near Vannes, later founding an important monastic school on the mainland close-by. It appears that he went on a visit to King Ainmire of Ireland in 560 AD and was an honoured guest at the monsteries of Bangor and Clonard.

Upon his return to Brittany he lived in a cave near the river Blavat at Larmor, though he died on the island of Houat. His shrine can still be seen in the church of St-Gildas-de-Rhuys in the Morbihan region; his holy well stands about one mile away. St Gildas the Albanian is probably the same saint, this name implying his northern (Scottish) origin.

ST GLYWYS, Glywyatus, Glivis or Gluvais, died 560, Monk and Martyr, 3rd May. Born in Wales son of St Gwynllyw (Woolos), and brother of St Cadoc. He founded churches at Coed-Kernew near Newport in Gwent and Merthyr-Glivis (Llandanglwys) in Mid Glamorgan, where his shrine attracted pilgrims. The place-name Merthyr-Glivis suggests that he met a martyr's death there, but more likely he went with his nephew St Petroc to Cornwall, where churches are named after him at St Gluvais and Penryn.

ST GOVAN, Gowan, or Gobhan, died 586, Abbot, 26th March. He was apparently an Irishman and a disciple of St Ailbeus (Elvis). Gobhan (Govan) founded and became abbot of a monastery at Dairinis-Insula (530) near Wexford, and has church dedications at Portbraddan and Craigavon in Ireland. He came as a missionary to south-west Wales in old age and lived there as a hermit in Pembrokeshire, at what is now St Govan's Head near Bosherston. Here he built himself a hermit's cell with an adjoining chapel by the precipitous cliffs of Stack Rocks.

The present St Govan's Chapel was rebuilt in the thirteenth century; inside, it measures eighteen feet by twelve, and has a vaulted roof and a stone altar, under which legend has it that the saint is buried. St Govan's Cell is located behind the altar in the cleft of a rock. The massive boulder which forms the hermit's cell has grooves carved into it, which were perhaps made by St Govan's fingers; some even say he was a giant! The chapel once had a bell on its roof, but this was lost to the sea. St Govan's holy well (Ffynnon Govan) stands just below the chapel amongst some rocks, sadly it is now dry, but up to the nineteenth century, pilgrims came here to seek a cure; failing eyesight was restored and cripples walked again after drinking the water; crutches were left there as a votive offering. Red soil from around the chapel was made into poultices and used to cure sore eyes, and it is said still to work today!

It is difficult to count the exact number of steps that lead to St Govan's Chapel; if they are counted on the way down, and again on the way up, a different number is reached, but there are between sixty and seventy.

Very little is known about St Govan, though he may have been a disciple of St David. One somewhat romantic legend associates the chapel with King Arthur's knight, Sir Gawain, who is said to have retired there after Arthur's death. There is a place called Llangovan in Gwent which may perhaps be named after this saint.

ST GWEN or Wenn, died 544, 18th October. Born in south-west Wales, daughter of Cynyr a chieftain of Pembrokeshire. She was the sister of St Non (mother of St David) and a granddaughter of King Brychan Brycheiniog. Gwen went to Cornwall and married St Selyf, who succeeded his father Geraint as King of Cornwall and Devon; St Cybi was their son.

Both Gwen and her husband King Selyf founded each their own churches and they were highly respected Christians in the south-west of England. St Gwen founded the church of St Wenn near Bodmin; she has one other dedication at Morval near Duloe. St Selyf (Selevan) has a church named after him at Lansallos near Fowey, and he is patron saint of St Levan in Cornwall.

ST GWEN, died 492, Martyr, 18th October. She is often confused with St Gwen above for she was Welsh and also one of the children of King Brychan. According to legend she led a very saintly life at Talgarth (Garth Madrun) in Powys, where Brychan held his royal court. There she was murdered by heathen Saxons who had invaded the area. Later a church was built there and a shrine erected to house her body. A church is still dedicated to her at Talgarth, and she has one other dedication at nearby Llyswen. She was mother of Caradog Freichfras, a knight of King Arthur. She is known as St Gwen of Talgarth, to distinguish her from St Gwen of Cornwall above.

ST GWENFYL, died 5-6c, Virgin and Nun, 1st

November. Little if anything is known about her except that she was the sister of St Callwen, and settled at or near Llandewi Brefi in Dyfed.

ST GWLADYS, or Gladys, died 6c., nun, 29th March. A daughter of King Brychan. She married St Gwynllyw (Woolos) king of Gwent; her five children are known to us as SS Cadoc, Cyfyw, Cynidr, Glywys and Maches. After the conversion of her husband to Christianity, she went to live at Pont Ebbw near Newport and then became a nun at Pencarn in Bassalag, a nunnery which was perhaps founded by her. Capel-Gwladys near Gelligaer in Mid Glamorgan was built by St Gwladys in the early sixth century. The church ruins there were discovered in the early twentieth century along with an ancient incised stone cross, now in Gelligaer church.

ST GWYNLLYW, Gundleus, or Woolos, died 523 King, 29th March. He was the son of King Glwys or Glewisseg. Upon his father's death he became king of Gwynllwg = Wentlooge, an area from the river Usk at Newport to the Rhymney at Cardiff. He married St Gwladys daughter of Brychan, and they had at least five children (see above). One of the sons, Cynidr, built a church at Llangynidr and a monastery at Glasbury in Powys; another Glywys is associated with Coed-Kernew, and their daughter, Maches, with Llanvaches in Gwent.

Gwynllyw lived a life of wickedness and violence towards his enemies. He did not care about anyone nor anything; only himself. His wife and children prayed to God for him to be converted to the Christian faith, but without success. One night, however, he had a dream in which he was told to seek a certain hill where he would find a white ox. Next morning Gwynllyw did as the voice had commanded, knowing it was the voice of God. Soon he found the white ox standing on

Stow Hill. In 500 AD he built a church on that same hill, where Newport Cathedral now stands dedicated to him. Gwynllyw and his wife began to live ascetic lives; often they would bathe both day and night in freezing cold water, though their son Cadoc quickly put an end to this. After his death, St Gwynllyw was buried in his own church at Newport in Gwent. He has one other dedication at Ystradgynlais in southern Powys.

ST GWYNNOG, Wennog, or Wynnoc, died 580, Abbot, 26th October. He was a son of St Gildas. He founded the first church of Llanwnog near Newtown in Powys, but probably not the church of Llanwenog in Dyfed.

He and his father stayed with St David, and then journeyed to Clonard in Ireland to seek a wider knowledge of the monastic way of life. But later he came to Cornwall and visited his aunt and uncle SS Wenappa and Enoder, who have church dedications there.

In 540 AD he became a missionary in Brittany and founded a monastery at Gouesnou near Brest. In later life, Gwynnog retired to Quimperle; he seems to have been killed when a hammer fell on him from a scaffold during the building of his church there. He has often been confused with two other saints of this name - St Gwynog of Pumpsaint in Dyfed, and St Gwynnoc or Winnoc (died 717) who founded a monastery at Wormhout in France.

ST HELEN (Elen Luyddoc) of Caernarfon, died 5c, Widow, 22nd May or 25th August. There has been much confusion between this Helen and St Helen (died 330) the mother of Constantine the Great. The mix-up arose because the Welsh Helen also had a son called Constantine. She was the daughter of King Eudaf who apparently ruled Ewyas (part of west Herefordshire). According to legend, she led an army into North Wales and later settled at Caernarfon where her father was a landowner.

When the Roman governor Magnus Maximus (Macsen Wledig) and his army came to Wales in 383 AD he was elected emperor by his own soldiers. One night he had a dream about a beautiful Welsh girl called Helen; so next morning he re-traced the path shown in his dream. Very soon he arrived at Caernarfon in North Wales and found Helen, the girl of his dream. Maximus and Helen were married, and as a wedding gift, Maximus gave his wife the fortifications of Caerleon, Caernarfon and Carmarthen.

Two of their sons are known to us today as St Constantine or Gasteynin and St Publicus (Peblig). They both have church dedications - St Gasteynin at Llangwstenin near Colwyn Bay, Welsh Bicknor (Llangystenin) in Herefordshire and Llangasty-Talyllin in Powys, and St Peblig at Llanbeblig, which is on the outskirts of Caernarfon. When Maximus left Wales with his legions, he was accompanied as far as Trier by Helen. However, shortly after his return to Rome he was murdered at Aquileia in Italy (388 AD).

It seems that Helen and her sons travelled back through Gaul, visiting Tours on the way, and probably returning to Wales. She was renowned for her kindness and charity to others - being regarded after her death as a saint. St Helen's holy well is located in South Street at Coed Helen in Caernarfon. Churches at Llanellen in Gwent, and Llanelen in West Glamorgan, are dedicated to her. The ancient Roman road called the Sarn Helen in Wales often attributed to her, can still be found in parts of Gwynedd, Powys and West Glamorgan.

ST HENWYN, Hywyn, or Ewyn, died 6c, Abbot, 1st or 6th January. He was a Welsh monk of Llanilltud-Fawr, and founded the church at Aberdaron in Gwynedd. Henwyn became Abbot of Bardsey Island.

ST ILLTUD, Illytud, Illtyd, or Elltud, died 530, Abbot, 6th November. It has often been suggested that St Illtud was born in Brittany, but he was very likely born in Breckonshire, Wales, about the year 450 AD. His parents, however, were Bretons who had migrated to Wales.

As a young man Illtud entered into the service of his cousin King Arthur and became a knight; then Arthur asked him and two other knights to look after the Holy Grail. But shortly after, his life changed when some close friends were killed during a hunting accident. Illtud was terribly shocked by this, and vowed to change his life. A local holy man told him to give up his worldly life, so he went with his wife to live beside the river Nadafan. Here he was visited by an angel and instructed to seek a more solitary life, so he became a hermit by the river Hodnant in South Glamorgan. Later he met St Garmon and they founded a monastery afterwards called Llanilltud-Fawr, and more recently Llantwit-Major. The exact date of the foundation of Illtud's monastery is uncertain, but it was probably sometime between 470-480 AD; certainly it was flourishing by 500 AD under Abbot Illtud, and many well-known saints were among his pupils, including David, Gildas, Padarn, Paulinus and Samson.

Illtud was a very learned man who had the knowledge of philosophy, poetry, scripture and, not least, rhetoric. He was a kind and holy person with the gift of prophecy.

His disciples were renowned missionaries; they preached in Wales, Cornwall and Brittany. A vast number of churches were founded by Illtud, and they include: Llantrissant and Llantwit-Fardre, Mid Glamorgan, Llanhamlach in Powys, Ilston, Llanrhidian, Oxwich and Pembrey in West Glamorgan; also Llanhilleth and St Illtyd in Gwent. He has two other more distant church dedications at Llanelltyd in Gwynedd, and on Caldey Island where he founded a monastery in conjunction with St Samson, who became second abbot after St Pyro.

In later life he went to distribute corn to the starving in Brittany, and also built churches at Aber-Ildut and Lanildut. St Maudet's Church at Landebaeron in Finistere possesses a silver reliquary which contains the so-called skull of St Illtud.

He probably died at his monastery in South Glamorgan around the year 530 AD, or perhaps as late as 545 AD. It is possible, however, that he died at Dol in Brittany while visiting St Samson. It is also possible that he was buried at Bedd-Gwyl-Illtyd near Brecon; the church of Llanilltud at Libanus half a mile away, bears his name.

According to legend it was St Illtud who introduced a new method of ploughing into Wales, no doubt he put this to good use on the land surrounding his own monastery.

In the church of St Illtud at Llantwit-Major is a collection of Celtic memorial stones - the Illtud Cross Shaft, the ninth-century Wheel Cross of Houelt, and St Samson's Pillar Cross. A holy well is named after Illtud at Llanrhidian, West Glamorgan.

ST ILLUDIANA, Juliana, Juliot, or Julitta, died 5-6c, Martyr, 29th June. A daughter of King Brychan of Brecknock, it seems she is to be identified with St Julitta (Juliot) of Llanilid in Mid Glamorgan, who in 500 AD was the founder of a monastery at Tintagel Head in Cornwall, the remains of which can still be found on the cliffs close to the ruins of Tintagel Castle.

The church at St Juliot in the Valency Valley is dedicated to her, and Luxulyan Church may also bear her name. Apparently St Julitta was murdered at Luxulyan by a robber who had already stolen from her. However the church there seems to be dedicated to the early fourth-century Roman martyrs SS Cyricus and Julitta, but there is still some confusion between St Illudiana and St Juliot, as to whether they are in fact one and the same person.

ST ISHMAEL, Ismel, Issel, or Ysfael, died 605, Bishop, 16th June. The son of Budic, prince of Brittany, and brother of St Oudoceus. Prince Budic and his family were exiled to Wales, though they were soon able to return to their native Brittany. Ishmael and his brother came back to Wales in order to be educated; Ishmael later became a disciple of St David.

He founded the church of St Ishmael's near Milford Haven in Dyfed, and has church dedications at Llanismel and Camrose in the same county, as well as St Ishmael near Kidwelly. The churches at St Isell's (Haroldston) and Saundersfoot in Dyfed are probably also named after him.

According to legend, he accompanied St David on a pilgrimage to the Holy Land. Ishmael was later consecrated bishop by his nephew St Teilo, and upon the death of St David he became Bishop of Menèvia (Mynyw). But the authenticity of this saint is questionable.

SS JULIUS AND AARON, died 304, Martyrs, 1st July. All that is known about them is that they were citizens of Chester. After being converted to the Christian faith they suffered as martyrs at Caerleon. A church at Newport in Gwent is dedicated to them.

ST JUSTINIAN, died 540, Hermit and Martyr, 23rd August or 5th December. He was born in Brittany of noble parentage and was divinely commanded to give up his worldly life. He became a priest, and then accompanied a band of missionaries to Wales.

On reaching Ramsey Island (Ty Dewi) he became a hermit and built himself a chapel, of which only a few foundation stones remain. Ramsey Island had, however, been occupied in the third century by St Devynog (Tyfynog), one of the first Christian hermits in Wales. Justinian began to work the land and asked the local people to help him; and so they did, but this was not a good idea in the long run, as we shall see. Later, he became the friend and confessor of St David, and was given some property on the mainland and also on Ramsey Island.

Now Justinian began working the locals much harder, and even disciplined them. When visitors kept coming to his island, he prayed that the causeway linking it with the mainland would disappear, which it did; only some submerged rocks (called The Bitches) now remain.

According to legend, Justinian was tricked by some sailors; they informed him that David was very ill and needed to see him, so he set sail with them, but soon realized they had tricked him. When he reached St David he found him to be quite well. He returned to his cell on Ramsey Island, but one day three of his servants who were friends of the sailors, took revenge on him because they did not like his severe disciplinary ways. They went mad with rage, pushed the holy man to the ground, and beheaded him. Where his head fell, a spring of water gushed forth from the ground. Justinian's decapitated body then "glided" across Ramsey Sound to Porthstinian where another holy well sprang forth, now called St Justinian's Well and located directly across from the chapel in the direction of the Lifeboat Station. St Justinian's roofless chapel (rebuilt 1515) by Bishop Vaughan, marks the place where the saint was first buried, before his body was taken by St David to his monastery church; St Justinian's relics are now in St David's Cathedral.

A church at Llanstinan near Fishguard is dedicated to him. He is probably not the same person as St Iestyn of Llaniestyn, Anglesey, who is depicted on a carved stone inside the church.

ST KENTIGERN, or Cyndeyrn, died 603, Bishop, 13th or 14th January. According to legend he was the illigetimate son of St Thenew (Thenoga) daughter of the king of Lothian. The king refused to accept his daughter's strange, even miraculous pregnancy, so he had her thrown over a cliff into the Firth of Forth in Lothian. Miraculously, her coracle came to rest safely at Culross near Dunfermline in Fife. Here St Thenew gave birth to her son, and later she took him to St Servanus (Serf) who ran a monastic school at Culross; he then brought up and educated young Kentigern. Eventually Kentigern became a priest, and first Bishop of Glasgow. When he began to suffer from political persecution, he fled to Cumbria and Wales.

In Cumbria he built some churches, including Dearham and Great Crosthwaite.

In North Wales he settled by the River Elwy, where he met a young boy called Asaph. Together they founded a monastery about the year 550 AD; the town of Llanelwy (renamed St Asaph in the twelfth century) grew up around this monastery, which Kentigern had handed over to St

Asaph.

Very little else is known about St Kentigern's (Cyndeyrn's) mission to Wales; however he has a church dedication at Llangendeirne near Carmarthen in Dyfed; possibly he founded a church or a monastery there. It is said that he met St David during his sojourn in Wales.

On his return to Strathclyde at the request of King Rederech (Rydderch), he took up his former duties as Bishop of Glasgow. St Kentigern died at Glasgow, or perhaps at Hoddam in Dumfries.

Numerous legends and miracles were ascribed to him including being rescued from drowning by an eagle, and restoring St. Serf's pet robin to life; there is also the tale of a lost ring being found in a salmon (told also of St Asaph). In Scotland he is affectionately known as St Mungo - "Darling."

ST KEYNE, Keyna, Cain, Cenau, or Cenedlon, died 490 or 505, Virgin, 8th October. She was born in Wales a daughter of King Brychan. She grew up to be very beautiful, and many young men sought her hand in marriage, but she rejected them all. Eventually she took a vow of virginity and became a nun. Shortly after, she set sail across the Bristol Channel and built her cell where the village of St Keyne, in Cornwall, now stands. Her holy well is about half a mile south of the village; according to legend, the first one of a newly-married couple to drink at the well will be master for life.

Keyne visited St Cadoc at St Michael's Mount in Cornwall, and he told her to return to Wales, which she agreed to do. In 480 AD she settled beside a hillock near Crickhowell in Powys, at a place which is nowadays called Llangenny. It was there that her prayers caused a holy spring to burst forth from the ground, and by it she founded a chapel. The chapel was demolished in 1790, but the holy well remains.

She told St. Cadoc when he was visiting her at Llangenny, that her abode would one day fall into the hands of sinful people, but that others would root them out, and by her prayers they would find her tomb, which would be in a place where the Lord's name would be blessed forever. She founded the church of Llangeinor in mid Glamorgan and also has church dedications at Llangunnor and Llangain in Dyfed, at Rockfield (Llangenon) in Gwent, as well as Runston church (now ruined) also in Gwent. Keynsham in Somerset is seemingly not named after St Keyne, but after a local Saxon saint called Kaegin or Caega.

ST KYWERE, Kiwa, or Kew, died 5-6c., Abbess, 8th February. All that is known about her is that she was perhaps born in south-west Wales and was the sister of St Cyngar (Dochau). It could be that she visited Ireland, though her cultus seems to have been mainly in Cornwall. Kywere founded a nunnery at St Kew near Padstow; the church there used to be named after her brother Dochau or Docco, but in the middle-ages she became its patron saint.

ST LEONORIUS, or Lunaire, died 570, Abbot and Bishop, 1st July. He was born in Wales of noble parents and educated by St Illtud at Llanilltud-Fawr in south Glamorgan. Later he became a missionary in Brittany and founded a monastery at Pontual; he possibly became bishop of nearby St Malo.

ST LLAWDOG, or Llawdoc, died 6c? Confessor, 15th January. A Welsh monk who founded the church of Llanllawddog near Carmarthen. He also has a church dedication at Cilgerran, Dyfed.

ST LLECHID, or Leuchid, died 6c. Hermit, 2nd

December. He was a hermit at Llanlechid in Gwynedd. It appears that he was the son of King Ithael Hael and brother of St Gredifael (of Penmynydd, Anglesey), also of St Tegai, St Trillo and St Twrog.

ST LLIBIO, or Libio, died 590, Abbot, 28th February. Welsh monk and missionary in north Wales; disciple of St Cybi. He founded the church of Llanllibio in Anglesey.

ST LLILY, Lily, or Lilie, died 7c. Hermit, 3rd March. This particular saint has over the centuries been forgotten. He was a disciple of St David; seemingly he looked after St David when he was dying. A ruined chapel once dedicated to St Lily stood close to St David's cathedral.

ST LLIONIO, or Lionio, died 520, Confessor, 17th March. A Welsh monk who possibly founded a monastery at Llandinam in Powys, and has a church dedicated to him at Llanio in Dyfed.

ST LLUWCHAIARN, died 7c., Abbot, 11th January. He was probably a native of Wales and a disciple of St Beuno. The first church at Llanllwchaiarn in Powys was founded by him, and possibly also the church of Llanychaiarn near Aberystwyth in Dyfed.

ST LLYR, Llyre, or Lear, died 6c. Hermit, 27th October. Born perhaps in west Wales. He founded a monastery at Llanllyr in Dyfed, and a church at Llanilar south of Aberystwyth. The church of Llanyre in Powys may well be one of his foundations.

ST LLUD, or Ludd, died 5-6c. Virgin and Martyr, 9th October. She was one of the twenty-five saintly daughters of King Brychan Brycheiniog. According to legend Llud was murdered at Slwch Tump in Brecon, a hill which is some 247 feet high, and overlooks the town of Brecon in Powys. In the second and third century A.D. the hill was perhaps used as a fortification by the Romans, and later by the British.

St Llud was apparently beheaded by a Saxon chieftain, and where her severed head came to rest, a holy spring of water gushed forth from the ground - St Llud's well or Penginger well.

ST MABYN, or Mabene, died 6c. Nun, 18th November. She was a daughter of King Brychan and possibly became a nun in south Wales, though she is mainly remembered in Cornwall for her missionary activity. Mabyn founded the church of St Mabyn near Bodmin in Cornwall; perhaps she was a follower of St Kywere, who is venerated at the nearby village of St Kew. A stained-glass window at St Neot in Cornwall depicts St Mabyn.
ST MADERN, Matronus, or Madron, died 550, Hermit, 17th May. A Welsh monk and disciple of St Tudwall. He became a missionary to Cornwall and settled as a hermit near Lands End. The church and holy well at Madron in Cornwall are very probably named after him. St Madron's holy well is one mile north-west of the village and was once a place of pilgrimage due to the healing qualities of the water. The ancient chapel that stands close to the well has a stone altar inside, and water from the well enters the chapel through a passage in the wall.
ST MADOC, Maedoc, Maodhoge, Aedhan, or Aidan, died 626 or 632, abbot and bishop, 31st January. Born in the province of Connacht in Ireland. After a short period of education in Leinster, Madoc wished to become learned in the study of scripture, so he left his native land and came to Wales. He studied first under St David at Glyn Rhosyn and then under St Cenydd at Llangennith in west Glamorgan. After a few years he founded a monastery at Llanmadoc on

the Gower Peninsula; the church there is dedicated to him; churches at Llawhaden in Dyfed, and also Llanfadoc near Brecon in Powys, are named after him. St Madoc's holy well at Great Rudbaxton in Dyfed is located near the south wall of the church. It seems that Madoc became a follower of St David and, according to some, St David died in the arms of St Madoc.

After the death of St David, he became abbot of Glyn Rhosyn; however, later, he returned to Ireland and founded the monastery of Ferns in County Wexford, eventually becoming first bishop there. Madoc also built monasteries at Drumlane in County Cavan, at Rossinver in County Leitrim (where his holy well can still be seen), and at Clonmore in County Carlow, which was also one of his more famous monastic foundations, like that of Ferns.

St Madoc was known for his kindness to the poor; he gave away his and other people's clothes to those in need, and lived on bread and water for many years, though it seems he was none the worse for this!

Some of his relics and those of other Irish saints (including SS Berach, Brigid, Dymphna, Lachtin, Patrick and Senan) are in the National Museum at Dublin, whilst some other items associated with St Madoc (Maedoc) can be seen in Armagh Cathedral. He may be identical with St Aidan the founder of Llanidan old church in 616 A.D., near Brynseincyn, Anglesey. The church, now partly ruined, has a holy water stoup in the south porch which is always full of water despite droughts; the water had healing qualities. There is also a holy well in the garden of a nearby house.

ST MADRUN, Madryn, or Materiana, died 5c., nun, 9th April. She was probably born in south-east Wales, daughter of king Vortigern (Gwrtheyrn). Madron married king Ynyr Gwent who ruled the area from Caerwent to Raglan. She seemingly had three sons - Ceidio, Iddon and Tegern. According to legend she fled to Cwm Gwytheyrn on the Lleyn Peninsula, then to Carn Fadryn when a fierce battle broke out between king Vortigern and the pagan Saxons; in this battle Vortigern's son Vortimer was killed, and eventually too, king Vortigern himself died when his castle caught fire, or possibly he had killed himself.

The church at Rhodogeidio in Anglesey is probably dedicated to Madrun's son St Ceidio. Apparently Madrun built a nunnery at Trawsfynydd in Gwynedd; however later she went with her son Ceidio to Cornwall and settled at Minster where she founded a church and monastery. A church is dedicated to her and St Marcelliana at Tintagel Head, and St Madrun's (Materiana's) holy well stands close-by. St Madrun died and was buried at Minster.

ST MAGLORIUS, or Maeglor, died 575, Abbot, 24th October. A native either of Wales or Ireland and son of St Umbrafel, who was St Samson's uncle. He was educated by St Illtud at Llanilltud-Fawr (Llantwit Major) in south Glamorgan. Maglorius became a missionary with St Samson in Brittany and founded a monastery near Dol. In later life he retired to Jersey and just before his death he built another monastery on Sark. St Maglorius destroyed a fearsome dragon which had terrorized the people of Sark. His relics are still venerated in Paris.

ST MALO or Maclou, died 640, Bishop, 15th November. A Welsh monk (perhaps from Llancarfan) who became the apostle of Brittany. He founded the church of Aleth (St Malo) and was first bishop there. Malo is still honoured at Saintes in Brit-

ST MAWGAN
from stained glass at La Méaugon.

tany.

ST MAWGAN, or Maucan, died 5c., Abbot, 8th August. He appears to have been of Irish birth and was baptized by St Patrick. It was St Patrick who entrusted him with the Welsh mission and education of the clergy. Mawgan eventually set sail with his disciples, who included St Euny and St Torney (Tighernach); they however sailed on to Cornwall whilst Mawgan came to south-west Wales. According to tradition he founded a monastic school in south-west Wales, but the exact location is uncertain; it was possibly in the Cardigan area, or near Pembroke.

The possibility that as a boy St David was taught in Abbot Mawgan's monastery seems unlikely, though the legend says that it was in that monastery that St David received from God the gift of a white dove which would visit him and protect him.

Mawgan later went to Cornwall and founded the first church at St Mawgan near Newquay. A church at Mawgan near Helston in Cornwall may have been founded by him or by one of his many disciples. It could be that St Mawgan became bishop of the Scilly Islands.

ST MELANGELL, or Monacella, died 7c., Virgin, 31st January. She was perhaps an Irishwoman, though north Wales is sometimes claimed to be her native land. Her father was a certain king Cyfwlch Addwyn, who was related to St Helen of Caernarfon. Melangell fled from her father's court to avoid marriage and seek a life of solitude and prayer.

In the year 590 she settled in a wooded valley in north Wales and used a cave for her cell. One day prince Brochfael of Powys, the father of St Tysilio, came to hunt near her cave, accompanied by his hounds. It was not long before the

GWELY MELANGELL
after Baring Gould and Fisher.

prince and his hounds were in pursuit of a hare, but it managed to take refuge under St Melangell's robe, and when prince and hounds came upon this holy woman, they stopped in their tracks; the hounds would not kill.

Prince Brochfael was so taken aback by St Melangell that he asked her to marry him, but she said she could not as she only wanted to live her life for Christ. Later, the prince gave her some land upon which to build a monastery, in 604 A.D.; this place is today called Pennant Melangell, in northern Powys. Here St Melangell was well known for her kindness and saintliness.

Pennant Melangell church has many things of interest inside, such as St Melangell's stone shrine (from 1170) which can be seen in the 'Cell-y-Bedd' (Cell of the Grave) at the far end of the church; this was also the traditional site of her burial. Two fifteenth-century wood carvings depicting the legend of St Melangell and Prince Brochfael can also be seen on the loft screen. Today, St Melangell is patron saint of hares, known locally as St Monacella's little lambs.

ST MELLON, or Mallonius, died 314, Bishop, 22nd October. A Welshman who was born at Llanlleurog (now St Mellons) east of Cardiff. The church there is named after him. According to legend, he became first bishop of Rouen, France.

ST MENEFRIDA, or Mynver, died 5-6c., Nun, 24th November. Born in south Wales of the family of king Brychan Brycheiniog. It could be that she was associated with Minwear near Haverfordwest.

Menefrida, however, settled in Cornwall and became a nun at Tredresick near Padstow where a church and holy well bear her name. The village of St Minver just across the bay from Padstow also retains the name of this saint. According to local legend, St Menedfida was tempted by the devil, but she threw a comb at him, causing him to take flight to nearby Lundy Hole.

ST MERIADOC, or Meriasek, died 6c., Bishop, 7th June. A Welsh monk and missionary who has a church and holy well named after him at Cambourne in Cornwall. The famous Cambourne miracle-plays called 'Beunans-Meriasek' are performed in his honour.

He eventually settled at Salles near Vannes in Brittany, and founded a church there. Seemingly he became bishop of Vannes, but was later murdered by his two sons who disapproved of his religious fervour. His relics including his so-called skull survive in the church of Saint-Jean-du-Doigt at Salles.

ST MERRIN, Merryn, or Merin, died 6c., Monk, 4th April or 7th July. A Welsh monk who was a close relative of king Seithenin, and brother of king Einion and St Seiriol; also a cousin of St Tudno. Merin is associated with Bodferin in Anglesey; whether he is identical with Meirion, prince of north Wales who gave his name to Meirionethshire has not been established.

He became a missionary in Cornwall and founded the church of St Merryn near Padstow. His main missionary zeal was in Brittany; churches at Lanmerin and Plomelin are dedicated to him.

ST MEWAN, Mevan, or Meen, died 6c., Abbot, 21st June. He was probably born in south Wales where he became a monk and a disciple of St Samson. Later, he accompanied St Samson and another companion, St Austoll, to Cornwall. Mewan built a church at what is now St Mewan in Cornwall, and he is probably titular patron saint of Mevagissey near Gorran-Haven. He left Cornwall for Brittany, and there he founded a monastery in the forest of Broceliande; later he built a second foundation at the place now called St Meen near Rennes where he was abbot. He died at St Meen in the mid sixth century.

ST MORWENNA, Moorina, or Mwynenna, died 6c., Virgin, 5th or 6th July. One of the many daughters of king Brychan Brycheiniog, and aunt of St Clether (Cleer). She was possibly trained for the religious life in Ireland but is mainly remembered in Cornwall. In 500 A.D. Morwenna settled at Marhamchurch near Bude and founded her first church there, though later she travelled north to the place which is now called Morwenstow.

There the local people apparently helped Morwenna to build her church; she herself carried stone on her head from beneath the nearby cliff, and where she put some stones down in order to take a rest a spring of water gushed from the ground; this well (called St Morwenna's holy well) is located to the west of the church about halfway down the cliff.

The ancient font in Morwenstow church was often thought to have been built by the saint herself, but it probably dates from the tenth century. The people of Morwenstow and Marhamchurch still celebrate the miracles of St Morwenna, their patron saint, in a festival every year in the early part of August.

ST NECTAN, or Nighton, died 510, Hermit and Martyr, 17th June. The eldest son of king Brychan and uncle of St Clether. Nectan was probably trained for the monastic life in Ireland, but he has been confused with the Irish St Nechtan (died 7c) who built the church of Kilnaughton on the isle of Islay in Scotland; he accompanied St Columbanus to Gaul and then Italy.

The Welsh Nectan became a monk in south Wales, but in the year 500 he sailed with other members of his family to Padstow in Cornwall.

Later he became a hermit at St Nectan's Kieve or Glen, above a waterfall near Tintagel; he also lived from time to time at Hartland in Devon, a cell which he used whilst visiting his sister St Morwenna at Morwenstow; she would return his visit on the last day of each year.

One day Nectan met a swineherd who had waylaid some of his pigs, so the saint decided to find them, and in gratitude the swineherd's master presented Nectan with two cows. However the cows were stolen by robbers; when Nectan found the animals he chastised the robbers and tried to convert then to Christianity; for this they beheaded him. Legend says that St Nectan picked up his severed head and carried it for half a mile from Newton Cross to a well at Stoke near Hartland; this holy well (situated just off the main street) is still named after the saint, and the parish church at Stoke is dedicated to him. St Nectan's body was taken back to the Kieve near Tintagel and buried under the waterfall.

Another legend says Nectan on his deathbed threw his chapel bell into the waterfall and vowed that it would only reappear when the true religion was once again restored. In the eleventh century Nectan's relics were returned together with his gold staff to Stoke church. There is another St Nectan's holy well, inside a stone building, at Welcombe in north Devon. A church at St Nighton near Lerryn in Cornwall is also dedicated to him.

ST NENNOCA, Ninnoca, or Ninnocha, died 6c., Abbess, 4th June. A daughter of king Brychan, who became a missionary over in Brittany. She probably founded a monastery at Lanninoc and became abbess. There is much uncertainty as to whether Nennoca even existed, and it could be that Nennoca was a male saint. In parts of Brittany statues of this saint are still venerated.

TOMB OF ST NON
at Dirinon, Finistere.

ST NON, Nonna, or Nonnita, died 6c., 2nd or 3rd March. Daughter of Cynyr, prince of Pembroke and sister of St Gwen, also grand-daughter of king Brychan. She became, or was training to become, a nun at the monastery of Ty Gwyn near Whitesands Bay. It seems that she was seduced by prince Sant (son of king Ceredig), and became pregnant. Another legend says that Non was already married to Sant. She had to seek hiding; the legend says that she collapsed with labour pains during a violent storm. She pressed her fingers into a large boulder by her side, thus leaving her own finger impressions on the rock. The birth of the future patron saint of Wales, St David, took place in a sea of brilliant light, with lightning striking the boulder in two. St Non's chapel at Caerfai one mile south of St David's in Dyfed marks the spot where St David was born. The chapel (now ruined) is mediaeval, and inside stands an incised stone with a cross carved upon it. A more modern Roman Catholic chapel of St Non stands close-by.

St Non's well (beneath a stone hood) stands near the ruined chapel. The well was once famous for its healing qualities; nowadays people use it as a wishing-well; in the niche behind the well stands a statue of St Non, or is it the Virgin Mary?

David was baptized at nearby Porth Clais by St Albeus an Irish bishop, and at the very moment of his basptism a spring of holy water burst forth from the ground, this being one of his first miracles; reputedly the water cured the blind monk Mobhi.

Non brought her son up at Henfynyw near Aberaeron, and later with his help she founded a nunnery at nearby Llanon, where the church is dedicated to her. Two other Welsh churches are dedicated to her - Llannon in Dyfed, and Eglwys-

Nynnid in Glamorgan.

In later life she went to Cornwall and founded the church of Altarnon, at a place to which some oxen had pulled her portable altar-stone; Altarnon is thus derived from 'Altar of Non.' Near this church stands St Non's holy well; there is yet another well named after her at Pelynt near Fowey. A church at Bradstone in Devon is also dedicated to her.

St Non eventually settled at Dirinon (Dirinian) in Brittany where she probably founded a monastery. In the churchyard at Dirinon stands an ancient chapel and well dedicated to St Non, who is also called St Melaria in those parts; her tomb and altar-stone are preserved inside the chapel.

ST OUDECEUS, Ouduck, or Euddogwy, died 610 or 615, Bishop, 2nd July. He was the son of prince Budic of Brittany, but was probably born in south Wales, for his family migrated there about 550 A.D. Oudoceus was baptized by St Teilo his uncle, and educated at Llanilltud-Fawr in south Glamorgan.

Later, he founded the church of Llandogo near Tintern in Gwent. In 580 he became bishop of Llandaff succeeding St Teilo, though it may be more a question of bishop of Llandeilo-Fawr in Dyfed. According to legend he presented himself for consecration before the Archbishop of Canterbury. His shrine once stood in Llandaff cathedral; it disappeared in 1540, but the saint's chapel bell is still preserved there.

If we turn, however, to the results of modern scholarship, we find doubts expressed about this saint. Thus D. Simon Evans in his edition of G. H. Doble (Lives of the Welsh Saints) concludes Oudecus was a bishop who probably never had a cult as a saint in early times, and only came to be regarded as a saint after the production of the Book of Llandaff in the twelfth century.

ST PABO (Post Prydain), died 530, King 9th November. Son of king Coel Godebog of Strathclyde and St Cywair who was an Irish princess and the founder of the church of Llangower in Gwynedd. One of his more famous brothers was Llywarch Hen (Llywarch the Old), who is highly regarded amongst the Welsh bards.

Pabo married and had a son called St Dunwyd (Donat): he became the father of St Deiniol of Bangor. During his reign as king of the north Britons he led an army of warriors against the Picts in Anglesey about 500 A.D.; he won a great victory, sending the Picts back north again. Later, he became a monk in Anglesey and founded the church of Llanbabo.

St Pabo is depicted (in low relief) on a fourteenth-century stone in the wall of Llanbabo church, as a crowned king in royal attire with a sceptre; his name is carved on the stone.

ST PADARN or Patern, died 550, Abbot and Bishop, 15th April. He was probably born in Brittany the son of Pedradin ap Emyr Llydaw, though it has been conjectured that he was a native of south-east Wales because his family had come to those parts from Brittany. He has been confused with two Breton saints of the same name - St Paternus of Avranches (died 564) and St Padern, bishop of Vannes.

According to legend Padarn came to south Wales in 516 A.D. with his companions, St Cadfan, St Cynllo and St Tydecho. Then Padarn went for training to Llanilltud-Fawr before going north to found his famous monastery of Llanbadarn Fawr near Aberystwyth in Dyfed. His monastery soon became well-known as a centre of learning.

The church of St Padarn at Llanbadarn Fawr has two Celtic crosses in the south transept; the church probably stands on the site of St Padarn's early sixth-century monastery.

Padarn was given much of the land between the rivers Rheidol and Clorach by king Maelgwn Gwynedd, though this was only after the saint was found to be innocent of stealing royal treasure, and for restoring the king's failing eyesight.

Apparently Padarn was the first bishop of Llanbadarn Fawr, though there is some doubt that he in fact founded a bishopric there. He died at his monastery in 550 A.D., and was buried on Bardsey Island. Many churches are dedicated to him, including: Llanbadarn Fynnyd, Llanbadarn-y-Garreg and another Llanbadarn Fawr, in powys; also Llanbadarn Trefeglwys, Llanbadarn Odwyn, and Pencarreg in Dyfed. Llanberis church in Gwynedd is dedicated to him, and Dolbadarn nearby refers to the 'Meadow of Padarn.' The church at North Petherwin in Cornwall is dedicated to him.

ST PAULINUS, Pawl Hen, or Paul Aurelian, died 573, Bishop, 12th March (22nd Nov. in Wales). A Welsh prince who was born about 480 A.D., his father being a king or chieftain of British birth. It is uncertain as to just where Paulinus was born - possibly Brittany - though Wales is more likely, his parents having migrated there from Brittany.

When five years old Paulinus began his education at Llanilltud Fawr (Llantwit Major) under St Illtud, and he was joined there by Gildas and Samson. He became a hermit near Llandovery and also built the church of Ystradffin nearby; the monastery of Llanddeusant (Two Saints) in Dyfed was founded by him, and probably named after two of his brothers; it became a famous school of monasticism. He seems to have spent some time on Caldey Island, and to have founded his own monastery at Ty Gwyn around 495 A.D., situated either north of St David's near Carn Llidi, or perhaps on the site of Whitland Abbey (Hendygwyn-ar-Daf). Here Paulinus was reputedly cured of poor eyesight by his pupil St David.

In the early sixth-century Paulinus went to Cornwall and stayed for a while with his sister St Sativola, founding a church at Paul near Penzance at the same time.

With twelve companions, mainly family and servants, he set sail for Brittany, landing on the isle of Ouessant or Ushant. Paulinus founded a monastery at Porz-Pol (Lampaul). Traditionally he became first bishop of the place now named after him, St Pol de Leon, after chasing away wild animals which had terrorized the local people.

In later life he retired to the island of Batz near Roscoff in Brittany, and built a monastery there on land owned by his cousin. Paulinus died there at an advanced age. His relics were given to the abbey of Fleury in 960, though some were returned to the city of St Pol de Leon and enshrined in the cathedral.

St Paulinus (Pawl Hen) is still venerated in Wales at Caldey Island and also at Ystradffin.

ST PETROC, Petrog, or Petrox, died 564, Abbot, 4th June. Born in south Wales the son of king Glywys of Glamorgan and Gwent, and probably trained for the monastic life in Ireland where he apparently stayed for some twenty-six years. On his return to Wales he founded a church at Llanbedrog on the Lleyn Peninsula in Gwynedd. Later Petroc travelled into south-west Wales where he has one other church dedication, at a place called St Petrox, near Pembroke in Dyfed.

In 500 A.D., he went on pilgrimage to Rome, returning later to Cornwall where he landed in the Hayle estuary. Upon his arrival in Padstow he found St Samson (or St Wethenoc) in residence. After a short dispute between the two, Samson went to Fowey. Petroc then built a church at Padstow (also known as Petrocstow) and shortly afterwards another at nearby Little Petherick together with his own mill. Then in 530 A.D., he became a hermit beside the river Camel at Bodmin, in a cell vacated for him by St Guron (Wyron) who moved on to Gorran Haven.

Bodmin was now the centre of his activities, and it was here that he founded his most famous monastery and where twelve disciples were to join him. But Petroc did live a very solitary life, though to compensate he was able to visit local villages and convert many to Christianity. According to legend, he gave shelter to a stag which was being pursued by a cruel huntsman; legend also says that Petroc once struck a rock with his staff in order to obtain water for thirsty harvesters.

He died at Treravel in Cornwall whilst on his way to visit one of his monasteries. Churches are dedicated to St Petroc at Holsworthy, Lydford, Newton-St-Petrock and Petrockstowe in Devon; those in Cornwall include St Petroc's Roman Catholic church in Padstow, and churches in Bodmin and Little Petherick.

In 1177 the relics of St Petroc were stolen from Bodmin church by a disgruntled canon who took them to St Meen in Brittany. However, king Henry II intervened, and the relics were returned to Bodmin church. An ivory casket containing the saint's relics was found over the porch of Bodmin church, and it is now regarded as one of the finest reliquaries in England. St Petroc is venerated in Brittany under the name St Perreuse.

ST SADWRN, died 6c., Abbot, 25th October. From

the very tiny shreds of evidence concerning this saint we can establish that he was a prince of Brittany who migrated to Wales, with his wife St Canna and his son St Crallo. It seems likely that Sadwrn went for training to Llanilltud-Fawr where his brother St Illtud ran a monastic school. Later, Sadwrn built the church of Llansadwrn near Llandovery in Dyfed.

However eventually he settled with his wife on the island of Anglesey; he has one church dedication at Llansadwrn on the island. A tombstone thought to be his stands in the chancel of Llansadwrn church, and is dated from 520 A.D.; it bears an inscription: "Here lies Saturnius and his saintly wife." This is perhaps the oldest memorial stone in Wales. Another tomb in nearby Beaumaris parish church is decorated on its sides with carvings representing St Sadwrn and St Canna, with Sadwrn apparently wearing armour complete with sheathed sword, while in his left hand he holds a pilgrim's staff; his right hand is poised in the act of giving a blessing, possibly indicating his conversion from a sinful life to that of a Christian one.

There is another saint of this name - St Sadyrnin (Saturnin) - who has a church named after him at Llansadurnen south-west of Carmarthen; possibly he was a missionary from north Wales.

ST SAMSON, died 565, Abbot and Bishop, 28th July. He was born in southern Wales in 485 A.D., son of Amwyn Dhu, a Breton chieftain. Amwyn came to wales and married Anna the daughter of king Meurig of Glamorgan. Samson was educated at Llanilltud-Fawr (Llantwit Major) in south Glamorgan where he was said to have been exceptionally quick in his studies, but austere in his ways.

He became a deacon and was ordained by St

Dubricius. Some of St Illtud's nephews had become jealous of Samson and tried to poison him, but the monastery cat drank the poison instead, so Samson went to Caldey island and was elected abbot there upon the death of St Pyro who had fallen into the monastery well after drinking too much wine. However, Samson failed to improve the bad habits of the monks at the monastery, so he decided to go to Ireland in order to re-form a monastery, and was accompanied by his father and St Umbrafel, his uncle.

On his return to Wales Samson retired with his father to a hermitage on the banks of the river Severn. One night he had a dream in which he was consecrated bishop by the holy apostles SS James, John and Peter. When Dubricius heard about this dream he asked Samson to prepare himself for consecration, but whether this was as abbot/bishop of Caldey remains uncertain.

He later went to Cornwall settling first at Padstow and then in the district of Trigg; he built churches at Southill and Golant (where he has a holy well), and sailed down the river Fowey with his disciples Austell and Mewan. Among the miracles attributed to him in Cornwall was his restoring to life a boy who had been thrown from his horse.

After settling in Brittany he founded a monastery at Dol; he also founded one at Pental in Normandy. From Dol he travelled to Guernsey where the town of St Sampson is named after him. In France, Samson obtained the release of the Breton prince Indual (Judual) restoring him to his people after he had been ousted by the infamous count Conmor.

In 560 A.D., king Childebert nominated Samson bishop of Dol, and he was consecrated shortly afterwards whilst in Paris. St Samson died peacefully at Dol in Brittany, though the Welsh have often claimed he died at Llanilltud-Fawr in south Glamorgan. Some of his relics are still preserved at Caldey abbey in Wales; whereas others can be found at Dol cathedral in Brittany.

Two legends concerning St Samson deserve a mention; one says a white pigeon landed on his shoulder whilst he was kneeling before the altar during ordination, and the pigeon wouldn't fly away until the ceremony had ended; another records how Samson instructed some noisy birds to be silent after they had annoyed his monks, and never again did they make such a noise. The Celtic cross of Samson can be found at Margam museum in west Glamorgan.

ST SEIRIOL, died 6c., Abbot, 1st February. A Welsh saint who has largely been forgotton. He was the son of Owain Danwyn, a descendant of Cunedda Wledig, and the brother of king Einion of Lleyn, prince Meirion of north Wales and prince Cynlas. In 510 A.D., king Einion and his brother prince Cynlas founded a monastery at Penmon in Anglesey and they installed Seriol as first abbot.

Two hundred yards north-east of Penmon priory, which was an Augustinian foundation built by Llewelyn the Great in 1221, is St Seiriol's holy well (Ffynnon Seiriol), and the saint's ruined hermitage stands close-by. The holy well is enclosed by an eighteenth-century stone building.

In the south transept of the priory church is a Celtic cross which dates from 1000 A.D., and an ancient font covered in carvings, as well as a stained-glass window depicting St Seiriol.

The nearby Puffin Island (Ynys Seiriol) was also inhabited by the saint in the sixth century, and some remains of a monastic church can still be seen on the island.

According to legend both he and St Cybi were

close friends and they would very often meet each other halfway across the island at the place called Llanerchymedd; there they would drink the water from a holy well and talk for several hours. A church is dedicated to St Seiriol at Penmaenmawr near Conwy.

ST SULIEN, Silian, or Tysul, died 6c., Confessor, 13th May. He was possibly a native of Brittany, although his family were related to king Cunedda of Wales, and St David was his cousin.

In the early sixth century Sulien came to Wales with a group of missionaries including SS Cadfan, Cynllo, Mael, Padarn and Tydecho (Tudec). After a short period of monastic training he went to visit his cousin St David (Dewi) and also founded the church of Llandyssul in Dyfed.

In the thirteenth-century church at Llandyssul is an altar stone with Celtic pattern-work carvings, and a picture of the crucifixion which depicts St John and the Virgin Mary.

Sulien became an ardent missionary in mid Wales, founding the churches of Capel-St-Silin near Lampeter in Dyfed, Llandyssil and Llansilin in northern Powys. He has church dedications (with St Mael) at Corwen and Cwm in Clwyd, but is very often confused with St Tysilio who has dedications in Anglesey, Clwyd, Powys, and at a few places in Dyfed.

In later life Sulien crossed over into Cornwall and may have founded the church of Luxulyan near Lostwithiel, though the church there has St Juliot (Julitta) as its patron saint.

It seems likely that St Sulien returned to Brittany and died there; churches in the western part of Brittany bear his name.

ST TEILO, Teilio, Telieu, or Eliud, died 560, Bishop, 9th or 13th February. Born at Penally in

Dyfed, son of St Mabon and St Tegfedd; also cousin of St Dubricius and uncle of St Oudoceus. He was educated by St David at Glyn Rhosyn and by St Paulinus at Llanddeusant near Llandovery, although it is sometimes claimed that he was educated by St Dubricius.

Teilo became a disciple of St David and accompanied him and St Padarn on a mythical pilgrimage to Rome and the Holy Land, where the legend states that they stayed for up to seventeen years. On his return to Wales Teilo founded his famous monastery of Llandeilo Fawr in Carmarthenshire (Dyfed), and this soon became the centre of his activities. From here he and his followers went out into what is now Powys, Gwent and Glamorgan, where he converted the people and built his churches.

In 545 A.D., Teilo went via Cornwall to Brittany in order to avoid the yellow plague; there he set up his mission centre at Landeleau, and founded churches at Pledeliac and St Thelo.

On his return to Wales in 550 A.D., he began to restore some of the monasteries (in what is now Herefordshire) that had earlier been built by St Dubricius. He is also said to have founded a church and monastery at Llandaff (on the site of the present Cathedral) and was, according to the 'Book of Llandaff' elected bishop there, but he was in fact abbot/bishop of Llandeilo Fawr.

St Teilo died around 560 A.D., at his monastery of Llandeilo. A dispute then arose between Llandaff, Llandeilo and also Penally as to whom should get his relics; to solve this problem, each place was given its own share. St Teilo's tomb is in the presbytery of Llandaff cathedral; his silver shrine (with his statue upon it) can be seen in the Lady chapel, (and there is a tenth-century cross in the south presbytery aisle).

Some twenty churches are dedicated to St Teilo, including: Llantilio Pertholey, Llantilio Crosseny and Llanarth in Gwent, Llandeilo'r Fan and Llandeilo Graban in Powys, Llandeilo Abercywyn, Llandeilo Llwydarth, Llandeilo and Penally in Dyfed. Two holy wells are named after him, they are located at Llandeilo Llwydarth (a famous healing well) in Dyfed, and another a few miles south of Peterston-Super-Ely in south Glamorgan. St Teilo's cross at Penally church in Dyfed probably marks the birthplace of this famous churchman. His mother St Tegfedd has a church dedication at Llandegveth (Llandegfedd) in Gwent.

ST TEWDRIC, or Theodoric, died 595, king and martyr, 1st April.

According to the Liber Llandavensis (or the Book of Llandaff) Tewdric was king of Morgannwg (Glamorgan).

In his old age he gave up his throne to his son, Meurig, and then retired to Din-Teyrin (Tintern) in Gwent, where he lived as a hermit. However, shortly afterwards, the area was invaded by pagan Saxons and Meurig sought his father's help.

Tewdric took up arms again to save the church from the Saxons, and it was not long before they took flight thanks to the courage of Tewdric and his son king Meurig. Tewdric however had been wounded in battle and his body had to be taken on a cart drawn by oxen. His people intended to take him to the tiny island of Flat Holm in the Bristol Channel, but the oxen suddenly halted at a spring of water and Tewdric's wounds were washed. There Tewdric died, and a church was built by his son Meurig to enshrine his father's saintly body; the place was eventually called Merthyr-Teyryn (Mathern) in Gwent.

St Tewdric's holy well in Mathern village is still

visited by the faithful, though the plaque gives Tewdric's year of death as 470 A.D., which is some one-hundred and twenty-five years earlier than the date generally given. In Mathern church a plaque on the north wall indicates the site of the saint's burial in 600 A.D. St Tewdric was possibly the founder of churches at Bedwas and Merthyr Tydfil, mid Glamorgan, and Llandow in south Glamorgan.

ST TRILLO, died 6c., Abbot, 15th June. A native of Brittany and son of Ithael Hael; his brothers SS Llechid, Tegai and Twrog have church dedications in north Wales. Trillo came to Wales probably with other missionaries and founded his church at Llandrillo-yn-Rhos in Clwyd (near the Gwynedd border).

His ancient chapel with a holy well inside is located by the sea shore on Marine Drive; the well once had healing qualities. Churches at Llandrillo near Corwen in Clwyd, and Llandrygarn in Anglesey bear his name. St Trillo was buried on Bardsey isle.

ST TUDNO, died 6c., Hermit, 5th June. Born in north-west Wales son of king Seithenyn and cousin of St Merin. Tudno was very probably educated in Ireland, but on his return to north Wales he became a hermit in a cave (Ogof Llech) on the coast near the Great Orme. Then later he founded a church a short way inland; the more modern church of St Tudno at Llandudno (the town is named after him) stands on the site of the saint's early church. Tudno was buried on Bardsey island (Ynys Enlli).

ST TUDWAL, Tugdual, or Tudwell, died 564, Bishop, 30th November or 1st December. The son of king Hoel (or Hael) and St Pompaea. Tudwal was trained in Ireland but became a monk in north Wales. He lived as a hermit on Ynys Tudwal (St Tudwal's Island East) off the Lleyn peninsula, where he founded a monastery; today only the ruins of his church and a priory can be found on the island. Another small island close-by is also named after him, as are the villages of Tudweiloig in Lleyn and Llanstadwell in Dyfed; churches there are dedicated to him.

In 545 A.D., Tudwal and his family went to Brittany and landed on the coast near Leon. Then shortly after Tudwal built a monastery at Lan Pabu on land granted to him by king Childebert I, but the king asked that in return Tudwal be installed as bishop over his people at Treguire; the saint agreed to do so, and he also founded the first church there.

He died at Treguire in Brittany and his shrine can still be seen inside the cathedral. According to one legend, St Tudwal was a kinsman of king Arthur. In art, the saint is often depicted as a bishop holding a dragon by his stole.

ST TUDY, Tudec, or Tydecho, died 560, Abbot, 11th May. Born probably in Brittany, though his family was related to the early Welsh kings; St Non (mother of St David) was his cousin.

He came to Wales with a group of missionaries and went firstly for training to Llanilltud Fawr in south Glamorgan, and then possibly to Ireland. Tudy (Tudec) took the gospel into Powys and built his first church at Mallwyd, then later he settled at Llanymawddwy in the valley of the Dyfi (Dovey) where he built another church on land granted to him by king Maelgwyn Gwynedd, although this was only after the two had quarreled. But Tudy was a kind and honest man; he got on well with the local people, and helped to farm the land.

One day king Maelgwyn told his men to stop ploughing the land. When they stopped, St Tudec continued ploughing his land with oxen pulling his plough. Maelgwyn told his men to train stags to till the land, and asked the saint to leave the area.

The following day while the king was out hunting he decided to take a rest on a limestone rock, but when he tried to get up again he found himself unable to move; Tudec arrived on the scene and performed a miracle, releasing him from the stone. The king was so grateful that he gave back the land to the saint. One other legend says that St Tudec cured the king's white horses of yellow fever, but asked that the king allow them to roam free; the king had to abide by this request.

Later, Tudec returned to Brittany via Cornwall; the church at St Tudy north of Bodmin is named after him. Seemingly he died on the Ile-de-Groix in Brittany; churches are decicated to him at Landudec and Loctudy in Cornouaille, also Port Tudy, Ile-de-Groix. Welsh accounts say he was buried on Bardsey Island along with SS Bodfan, Cadfan, Cynfelin, Dwywe, Gelynin, Padarn and Rhychwyn, who have churches in Gwynedd.

ST TYDFIL, died 460 or 480, Virgin and Martyr, 23rd August. She was born in Wales, a daughter of king Brychan. Tydfil lived as a hermitess at what is today the town of Merthyr Tydfil in mid Glamorgan. She was murdered there by pagan Britons, and a church was built on the site of her martyrdom. Her shrine once stood in the modern St Tydfil's church. One of her brothers St Cynog was also a martyr; he was murdered at Merthyr Cynog near Brecon in Powys. St Cynog's severed head rolled into a well which consequently dried-up.

ST TYSILIO, Sulio, or Suliau, died 640, Abbot, 8th November. There is uncertainty as to where

ST WINEFRIDE
after Baring Gould.

he was born, possibly Strathclyde in Scotland, but more likely north Wales. He was the son of Brochfael Ysgythrog, prince of Powys, grandson of St Pabo and cousin of St Asaph and St Deiniol. Tysilio became a hermit on Ynys Tysilio (Church Island) in the Menai Straits close to the Menai Suspension Bridge; a causeway links the island with the mainland, but a ruined fifteenth-century chapel on the site of the saint's cell is all that remains on the island.

However, from this island Tysilio evangelized Anglesey and even beyond; he founded the church of Llanfair P.G; or in its much longer form 'Llanfairpwllgwyngyllgogerychwyrndrobwllllandy-siliogogogoch' meaning 'St Mary's church in the hollow of the white hazel, near a rapid whirlpool and St Tysilio's church, near to a red cave.' The saint eventually established himself at Meifod in northern Powys where in 600 A.D., he built a monastery and church, next to a church founded earlier by St Gwyddfarch who had been a hermit at nearby Gallt-yr-Ancr (Rock of the Anchorite).

Tysilio even preached in south-west Wales; he has one church dedication at Llandissilio in Dyfed, with others at Llantysilio in Clwyd and Sellack in Herefordshire.

In the year 617 he went to Brittany and settled at a place now called St Suliac near St Malo, where he built a monastery. He died at St Malo (in 640) though this saint may be a different person, the Welsh St Tysilio dying perhaps at Meifod.

ST WINEFRIDE or Gwenfrewi, died 650, Abbess, 3rd November. She was born at Treffynnon - Holywell in north Wales, the daughter of Thewyth (Thenith ap Eylud) and Gwenlo. Winefride grew up into a very beautiful young woman and became well known to all the people of Treffynnon for her kindness.

One day a young prince called Caradoc ap alyn from Penarlag (Hawarden) came to her home; however both her parents were out attending mass in the nearby church, so Winefride found herself all alone. The prince started to seduce her but she ran quickly to the church; Caradoc came after her and once again attempted to seduce her, but she resisted. The prince now very angry took out his sword and beheaded Winefride; when her severed head made contact with the ground it caused a holy spring of water to burst forth. By now the congregation from the church had come to see what was going on; they saw Caradoc calmly wiping his blood-stained sword in the grass. St Beuno, Winefride's uncle, picked up the girl's head and began cursing prince Caradoc, at which the evil man sank into the ground and was never seen again. The girl was restored to life by St Beuno.

Thewyth entrusted his daughter to Beuno who gave her Christian instruction; eventually she went to St Elerius at Gwytherin near Llanwrst, and became abbess at a monastery built by him and his mother Theonia, who had been first abbess.

St Winefride died at Gwytherin and was buried in the church-yard; however in 1138 her relics were taken to Shrewsbury abbey. Her shrine there was destroyed in the sixtenth century, but a few of her relics remain in the abbey, and at a Roman Catholic convent in Holywell.

St Winefride's well at Holywell in Clwyd still draws a large number of people hoping to receive a miracle of healing, for certainly long ago the sick were cured there. Another St Winefride's holy well can be seen at Woolstan near Oswestry.

In the year 1500 Lady Margaret Beaufort, Countess of Richmond and Derby and mother of king Henry VII had a chapel built next to the well; she also built churches at Gresford, Northop (North Hope) and Mold in Clwyd.

ST WINNOC, Wynnoc, or Winnow, died 717, Abbot, 6th November. A Welsh monk who was often considered to have been the founder of the church of St Winnow near Lostwithiel in Cornwall. He became a missionary at St Sithiu (St Omer) in France, and was a monk at St Bertin's monastery. Later Winnoc founded his own monastery and church at Wormhout near Dunkirk; he died there in 717 A.D. A number of extraordinary miracles were performed by him.

2. Some other Saints of Wales
with their place of veneration.

ST AELEARN, 7c., hermit, and disciple of St Beuno. Llanaelhaearn in Gwynedd. 1st November.

ST BAGLAN, 6c., disciple of St Illtud. Llanfaglan, Anglesey, and Baglan in W. Glamorgan.
ST BEULAN, 6c., son of St Paulinus. Llanfeulan in Anglesey.
ST BILO (Milo), 5-6c., son of king Brychan. Llanfilo in Powys.
ST BODFAN, 6c., disciple of St Cadfan. Llanaber in Gwynedd.

ST CAFFO, 545, brother of St Gildas; martyr, Llangaffo, Anglesey.
ST CARON, 3c., Irish saint; king and bishop. Tregaron in Dyfed.
ST CAWDRAF, 6c., disciple of St Seiriol. Abererch in Gwynedd, and Llangoed in Anglesey.
ST CEIDIO, 6c., son of St Madrun. Ceidio (Rhodogeidio) in Anglesey.
ST CEINWR, 5c., great-grandson of king Carodoc. Llangeinwr in Gwent.
ST CIAN, 6c., monk and bard. Llangian near Abersoch in Gwynedd.
ST CYFYW, 6c., brother of St Cadoc. Llangyfyw in Gwent.
ST CYNFELIN, 6c., Breton missionary. Llangynfelin in Gwynedd.
ST CYNOG, 5-6c., son of king Brychan and martyr. Merthyr-Cynog, Llangynog and Defynnog in Powys; also Llangynog in Dyfed.

ST DUNAWD (Donat), 600; abbot and also father of St Deiniol of Bangor. St Donat's in south Glamorgan. 7th September.

ST DWYWE, 6c., disciple of St Cadfan. Llanddwywe in Gwynedd.
ST DYFAN, 2c., deacon. Llandyfan, Dyfed, and Merthyr-Dyfan, Glamorgan.

ST EDEYRN, 6c., son of king Vortigern. Llanedeyrn in S. Glamorgan.
ST EDEYRN, king and bard. Bodedern, Anglesey, and Edern in Gwynedd.
ST EDIE (Eddy), 6c., hermit. Llanedy near Ammanford in Dyfed.
ST EINION (Einiaun), 555, king of Lleyn. Llanengan in Gwynedd.
ST ELERIUS (Eleri), 7c., abbot and historian. Gwytherin, Gwynedd.
ST ELLYW, 6c., disciple of St Cadoc. Llanelieu in Powys. Llanelly in Gwent. Llanelli in Dyfed. St Ewe in Cornwall. 23rd January.
ST EURGAIN, 6c., daughter of king Maelgwn Gwynedd. Llaneurgain (Northop - North Hope) in Clwyd.

ST FILI, 6c., monk, son of St Cenydd. Caerphilly in mid Glamorgan; Rhosilli in west Glamorgan; Philleigh in Cornwall; Filleigh in Devon.
ST FFWYST (Foist), 6c., misionary from Anglesey. Llanfoist in Gwent.

ST GASTEYNIN (Cystenin or Constantine), 5c., son of St Helen of Caernarfon. Llangwstenin, Gwynedd; Llangystenin (Welsh Bicknor) in Herefordshire, and perhaps also Llangasty-Talyllyn in Powys.
ST GEINWEN, 5c., daughter of king Brychan. Llangeinwen, Anglesey.
ST GOVER (Gyfor), 6c., Llanover near Abergavenny in Gwent.
ST GREDFYN, 5-6c., Llanllyfni near Clynnog

Fawr in Gwynedd.
ST GREDIFAEL, 6c., brother of St Llechid. Penmynydd in Anglesey.
ST GWAUR (Cynwair), 6c., mother of St Pabo. Llangower in Gwynedd.
ST GWENFAEN, 6-7c., Welsh female saint. Rhoscolyn in Anglesey.
ST GWERFYL, 6c., Welsh princess. Bettws-Gwefil-Goch in Clwyd.
ST GWYDDFARCH, 6c., hermit and abbot. Meifod in Powys.
ST GWYNDAF, 6c., king. Llanwnda in Dyfed. Llanwnda in Gwynedd.
ST GWYNHOEDL, 600, monk. Llangwnnadl in Gwynedd.
ST GWYNNO, 529, abbot. Llanwonno in mid Glamorgan, Llanwinno in Dyfed, and Wonastow near Monmouth in Gwent. He is probably to be identified with St Winwaloe (Winnol) of Cornwall. 3rd March.

ST IDLOES, 7c., hermit. Llanidloes near Llangurig in Powys.
ST IESTYN (Jestin), 6c., son of Geraint. Llaniestyn in Anglesey, and Llaniestyn in Gwynedd. He may be the St Justin of Cornwall.
ST IGON (Egon), 5-6c., abbot. Llanigon near Brecon in Powys.
ST INA, 728, king of Wessex, and confessor. Llanina in Dyfed.
ST ISHAN (Isian), 6c., Llanishen in south Glamorgan; Llanishen in Gwent.
ST ISHOW (Issui), 6-7c., hermit and martyr. Partrishow in Powys.

ST KENEDER (Cynider), 6c., brother of St Cadoc and grandson of king Brychan. Llangynidr and Glasbury in Powys. 8th December.

ST LLAWEN, 6c., disciple of St Cadfan. Llanllawen in Gwynedd.
ST LLEWELLYN, 6c., Llanllowell (Llanllywel) Gwent. Llywel, Powys.

ST MACHES, 6c., sister of St Cadoc, and martyr. Llanfaches, Gwent.
ST MACMOIL, 6c., disciple of St Cadoc. Manmoel in Gwent.
ST MAEL, 6c., titular (with St Sulien) of Corwen and Cwm, Clwyd.
ST MAELOG (Meiliog), 590, abbot and brother of St Gildas. Llowes, Llandefalle, Llandefaelog Fach, Llandefaelog-tre-Graig in Powys, and Llandyfaelog in Dyfed; Llanfaelog in Anglesey.
ST MAETHLU, 6c., son of Caradoc Freichfras. Llanfaethlu, Anglesey.
ST MARCELLA, 5c? Denbigh (parish church - Eglwys Wen) in Clwyd, Capel Marchell (Llanwrst) Gwynedd, and Ystrad Marchell in Powys.
ST MEUGAN, 605, son of Gwandaf Hen. Llanfeugan in Powys, and Machen in Gwent; also Eglwyswrw (St Meugan's well) in Dyfed.

ST NIDIAN (Aidan, 7c., Irish bishop and disciple of St Kentigern. Llanidan in Anglesey.

ST PADRIG, 6c., abbot and disciple of St Cybi. He is probably not Patrick the Irish patron saint. Llanbadrig in Anglesey.
ST PEBLIG (Publicius), 5c., abbot and brother (or uncle) of St Gasteynin. Llanbeblig on the outskirts of Caernarfon in Gwynedd.
ST PEDORIC, 6c., disciple of St Dyfrig. Kilpeck in Herefordshire.
ST PERIS, 6c., friend and disciple of St Padarn. Llanberis and Nant Peris near Mount Snowdon in Gwynedd.
ST PYRO, 6c., abbot. Caldey Island, Dyfed; Machynys, west Glamorgan.

ST RHWYDRYS, 6c., hermit. Llanrhwydrys in Gwynedd.
ST RHYCHWYN, 6c., brother of St Celynin. Llanrhychwyn in Gwynedd.
ST RHYDIAN, 6c., Llanrhydian in west Glamorgan.
ST RHYSTUD (Gwrst), 5c., disciple of St Garmon. Llanwrst in Gwynedd, and Llanrhystud near Aberaeron in Dyfed.

ST SANNAN, 5c., bishop; Llansannan, Clwyd; Llantrisant, Anglesey.
ST SARAN, 5-6c., Irish saint; Llanynys near Denbigh in Clwyd.
ST SATURNIN (Sadurnen), 6c., bishop; Llansadurnen in Dyfed.
ST SAWEL, 6c., father of St Asaph. Llansawel in Dyfed.

ST TECWYN, 6c., disciple of St Cadfan; Llandecwyn in Gwynedd.
ST TEGAI, 6c., brother of St Llechid; Llandegai in Gwynedd.
ST TEGFEDD, 6c., mother of St Teilo; martyr; Llandegveth in Gwent.
ST TEGLA, 5c?, daughter of king Requli of Gwynedd, and martyr; Llandegley in Powys, Llandegla in Clwyd, Beachley (St Tecla's ruined chapel and holy well near the Severn Bridge) in Gwent.
ST TRITHYD, 6c., disciple of St Illtud; Llantrithyd in south Glamorgan.
ST TUDUR (Tudor), 5c., Welsh king (of Gwent); Mynyddislwyn, Gwent.
ST TUNABIUS (Dinabo), abbot; Llandinabo in Herefordshire.
ST TWROG (Turog), 610, disciple of St Beuno; Maentwrog near Ffestiniog in Gwynedd, and Llandwrog near Caernarfon in Gwynedd.

ST SANNAN
from stained glass in Llansannan Church.

ST TYBIE, 5-6c., daughter of king Brychan. Llandybie in Dyfed.
ST TYFODWG, 6c., Llandyfodwg, mid Glamorgan, and formerly Dixton in Gwent.

ST WEONARD (Gwenarth), 6c., hermit, Llanwenarth near Abergavenny in Gwent, and also St Weonards in Herefordshire.
ST WRW, 6c? female saint. Eglwyswrw, south of Cardigan, Dyfed.
ST WYDDELAN (Wyddel), 7c., disciple of St Beuno. Llanwyddelan in Powys, Llangwwddelan in Dyfed, and Dolwyddelan in Gwynedd.

MAP NO 1 WALES. THE MONASTIC SITES AND places associated with the saints of Wales.

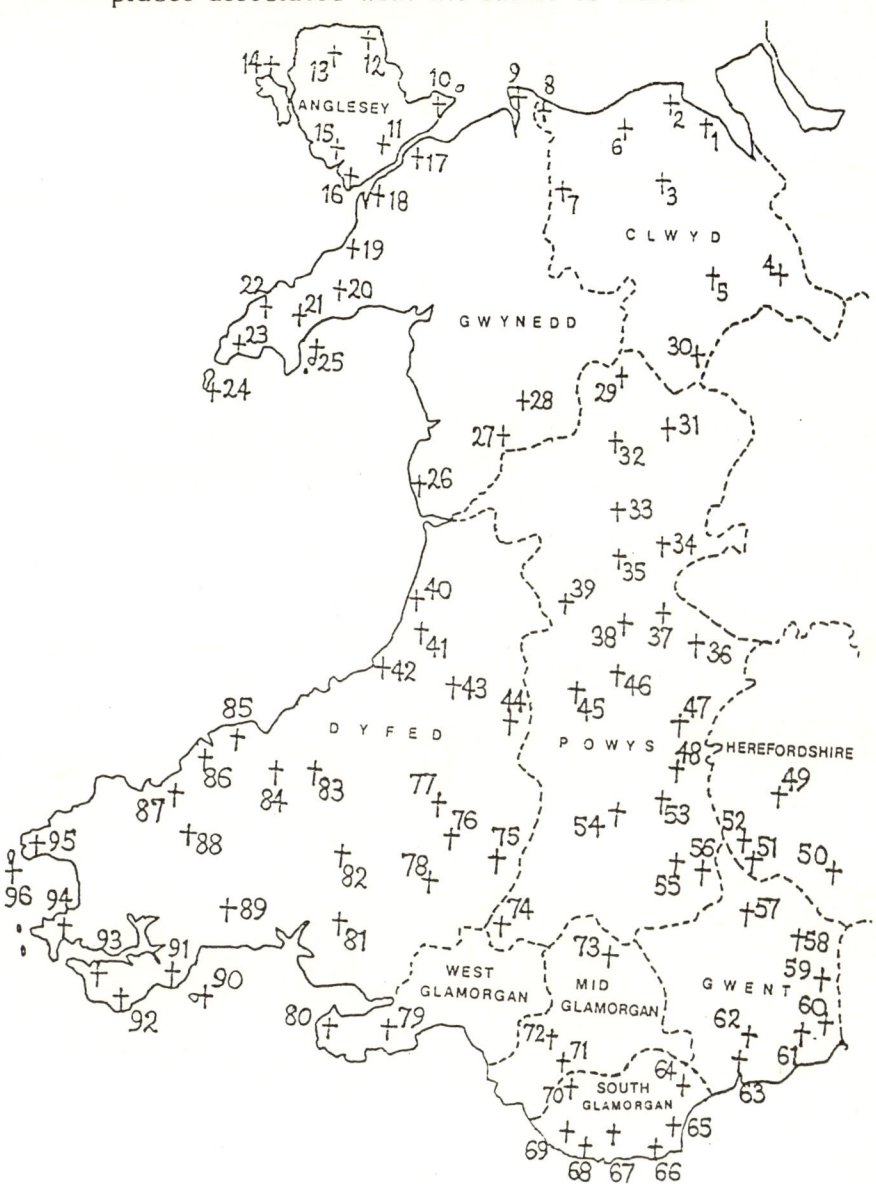

KEY TO MAP NO 1. THE MONASTIC SITES
and places associated with the saints of Wales.

1. Holywell (Treffynnon), Clwyd, St Winefride.
2. Llanasa, Clwyd, St Asaph.
3. Llangwyfan, Clwyd, St Cwyfan.
4. Bangor-on-Dee (Bangor Iscoed), Clwyd, SS Deiniol/Dunwyd.
5. Llangollen, Clwyd, St Collen.
6. St Asaph (Llanelwy), Clwyd, SS Asaph/Kentigern.
7. Gwytherin, Clwyd, SS Elerius/Winefride.
8. Llandrillo-yn-Rhos, Clwyd, St Trillo.
9. Llandudno, Gwynedd, St Tudno.
10. Penmon (Llangoed), Anglesey, St Seiriol.
11. Llanddaniel Fab, Anglesey, St Deiniol Fab (Deiniolen).
12. Llaneilian, Anglesey, St Eilian.
13. Llanbabo, Anglesey, St Pabo.
14. Holyhead (Caer Gybi), Anglesey, St Cybi.
15. Llangadwaladr, Anglesey, St Cadwaladr.
16. Llanddwyn (Llanddwyn Island), Anglesey, St Dwynwen.
17. Bangor (Bangor Fawr), Gwynedd, St Deiniol.
18. Caernarfon, Gwynedd, SS Helen/Peblig.
19. Clynnog Fawr (Lleyn Peninsula), Gwynedd, St Beuno.
20. Llangybi, Gwynedd, St Cybi.
21. Llanbedrog (Lleyn Peninsula), Gwynedd, St Petroc.
22. Tudweiliog (Lleyn Peninsula), Gwynedd, St Tudwal.
23. Aberdaron (Lleyn Peninsula), Gwynedd, St Henwyn.
24. Bardsey Island (Ynys Enlli), Gwynedd, St Cadfan & others.

25. ST Tudwal's Island East (off Lleyn Peninsula), St Tudwal.
26. Towyn (Tywyn), Gwynedd, St Cadfan.
27. Mallywd, Powys-Gwynedd border, St Tudec (Tydecho).
28. Llanymawddwy, Gwynedd, St Tudec (Tydecho).
29. Pennant Melangell, Powys, St Melangell (Monacella).
30. Llansilin, Clwyd, St Suilen (Silin).
31. Meifod, Powys, SS Gwyddfarch & Tysilio.
32. Llangadfan, Powys, St Cadfan.
33. Llanwnog, Powys, St Gwynnog.
34. Llanllwchaiarn, Powys, St Llwchaiarn.
35. Llandinam, Powys, St Llionio.
36. Llangunllo, Powys, St Cynllo.
37. Llanbadarn Fynydd, Powys, St Padarn.
38. St Harmon, Powys, St Garmonus.
39. Llangurig, Powys, St Curig (Cyric).
40. Llanbadarn Fawr, Dyfed, St Padarn.
41. Llanilar, Dyfed, St Llyr (Luyr).
42. Llanon, near Aberaeron, Dyfed, St Non (Nonnita).
43. Llandewi Brefi, Dyfed, St David (Dewi Sant).
44. Ystradffin, Dyfed, St Paulinus (Paul Aurelian).
45. Llanafan Fawr, Powys, St Afan (Avan).
46. Dysserth, Powys, St Cewydd.
47. Glascwm, Powys, St David (Dewi Sant).
48. Llowes, Powys, St Maelog (Meiliog).
49. Madley, Herefordshire, St Dubricius (Dyfrig).
50. Hentland (Henllan), Herefordshire, St Dubricius.
51. Clodock (Merthyr Clitauc), Herefordshire, St Clodock.
52. Llanveynoe (Llanfeuno), Herefordshire, St Beuno.
53. Talgarth (Garth Madrun), Powys, St Gwendoline.
54. Brecon (Brecknock), Powys, SS Brychan/Lludd.

55. Llangynidr, near Brecon, Powys, St Cynidr (Keneder).
56. Llangattock, near Brecon, Powys, St Cadoc (Cattwg).
57. Llanellen, Gwent, St Helen of Caernarfon.
58. Dingestow (Merthyr Dingat), Gwent, St Dingat.
59. Llandogo, near Tintern, Gwent, St Oudoceus.
60. Mathern, Gwent, St Tewdric (Theodoric).
61. Caerwent, Gwent, SS Athan & Cadoc.
62. Caerleon, Gwent, SS Aaron/Dubricius/Julian.
63. Newport, Gwent, SS Gwladys & Gwynllyw.
64. Llandaff, S. Glamorgan, SS Dubricius/Teilo/Oudoceus.
65. Llandough, near Cardiff, S. Glamorgan, St Dochau (Cyngar).
66. Barry Island, S. Glamorgan, St Barric (Barruc).
67. Llancarfan (Nant Carfan), S. Glamorgan, St Cadoc.
68. St Athan (Llandathan), S. Glamorgan, St Athan (Tathaneus).
69. Llantwit Major (Llanilltud Fawr), S. Glamorgan St Illtud.
70. Llangan, S Glamorgan, St Canna.
71. Coychurch, Mid Glamorgan, St Crallo.
72. Llangeinor, Mid Glamorgan, St Keyne (Cenau).
73. Merthyr Tydfil, Mid Glamorgan, St Tydfil.
74. Ystradgynlais, Powys, St Gwynllyw (Woolos).
75. Llandeussant, Dyfed, St Paulinus (Paul Aurelian).
76. Llansadwrn, Dyfed, St Sadwrn.
77. Pumpsaint, Dyfed, SS Ceitho/Celynen/Gwyn/Gwynaro/Gwynog.
78. Llandeilo (Llandeilo Fawr), Dyfed, St Teilo.
79. Ilston (Iltwitson), W. Glamorgan, St Illtud.
80. Llangennith & Llanmadoc, W. Glamorgan, SS Cenydd & Madoc.
81. Llangendeirne, Dyfed, St Kentigern (Cyndeyrn).
82. Llanlawddog, Dyfed, St Llawdoc.
83. Llandyssul, Dyfed, St Tysul (Sulien?).

84. Llandyfriog, Dyfed, St Brioc.
85. Llangranog (Llangrannog), Dyfed, St Carranog.
86. St Dogmaels (Llandudoch), Dyfed, St Dogmael.
87. Nevern, Dyfed, SS Brynach & Clether.
88. Llangolman, Dyfed, St Colman of Dromore.
89. Whitland (Hendygwyn-ar-Daf), Dyfed,
St Paulinus.
90. Caldey Island (Ynys Pyr), Dyfed,
SS Illtud/Pyro/Samson.
91. Penally, near Tenby, Dyfed, St Teilo.
92. St Govan's Head, near Bosherston, Dyfed,
St Govan.
93. Rhoscrowther (Llandegyman), Dyfed,
St Decuman.
94. St Ishmael's, near Sandy Haven, Dyfed,
St Ishmael.
95. St David's (Ty Dewi), Dyfed,
SS Caradoc/David/Justinian.
96. Ramsey Island, Dyfed, SS Devynog & Justinian.

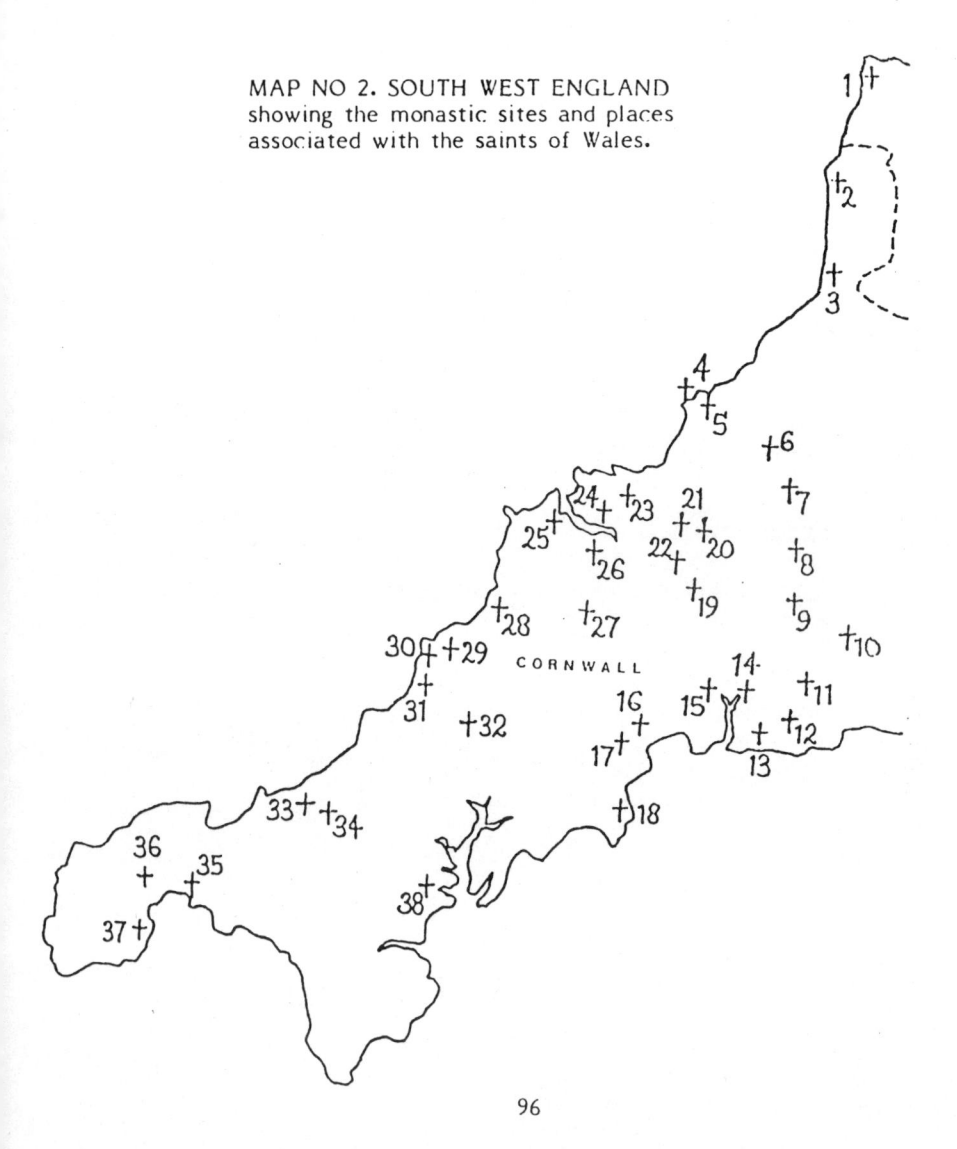

MAP NO 2. SOUTH WEST ENGLAND
showing the monastic sites and places
associated with the saints of Wales.

KEY TO MAP NO 2. SOUTH WEST ENGLAND THE MONASTIC SITES AND PLACES associated with the saints of Wales.

1. Stoke and Hartland, North Devon, St Nectan (Nighton).
2. Morwenstow, Cornwall, St Morwenna (Mwynen).
3. Marhamchurch, near Bude, Cornwall, St Morwenna (Mwynen).
4. Tintagel Head, Cornwall, SS Juliot & Madrun (Materiana).
5. St Nectan's Kieve (Glen), near Bossiney, Cornwall, St Nectan.
6. St Clether, Cornwall, St Clether (Cleer).
7. Altarnun, Cornwall, St Non (Nonna).
8. St Cleer, north of Liskeard, Cornwall, St Cleer (Clether).
9. St Neot, Cornwall, St Neot.
10. St Keyne, south of Liskeard, Cornwall, St Keyne.
11. Duloe, near Morval, Cornwall, St Samson.
12. Pelynt, west of Looe, Cornwall, St Non (Nonna).
13. Lansallos, east of Fowey, St Selyf (Selevan).
14. St Nighton, near Lerryn, Cornwall, St Nectan (Nighton).
15. Luxulyan, Cornwall, SS Illudiana (Juliana) & Sulien.
16. St Austell, Cornwall, St Austell (Austoll).
17. St Mewan, near St Austell, St Mewan (Mevan).
18. Mevagissey, north of Gorran Haven, Cornwall, St Mewan.
19. Bodmin, Cornwall, SS Guron & Petroc.
20. St Tudy, Cornwall, St Tudy (Tudec).
21. St Kew, south of Pendoggett, Cornwall, St Kew (Kywere).
22. St Mabyn, near Wadebridge, Cornwall, St Mabyn.

23. St Endellion, west of Pendoggett, Cornwall, St Endelienta.
24. St Miniver, north-east of Padstow, Cornwall, St Menefrida.
25. Padstow (Petrocstow), Cornwall, St Petroc.
26. St Breock, near Wadebridge, Cornwall, St Breock (Brioc).
27. St Wenn, Cornwall, St Wenn (Gwen).
28. St Mawgan, Cornwall, St Mawgan (Maucan).
29. Crantock, near Newquay, Cornwall, St Carantoc (Carannog).
30. Cubert, south-west of Newquay, Cornwall, St Cuby (Cybi).
31. Perranporth, Cornwall, St Piran (Perran).
32. St Allen, north of Truro, Cornwall, St Allen (Alun, Ailen).
33. Camborne, Cornwall, St Meriadoc.
34. Gwenap, near Redruth, St Gwenappa (Wynup).
35. St Michael's Mount, Cornwall, SS Cadoc & Keyne.
36. Madron, Cornwall, St Madron (Madern).
37. Paul, near Penzance, Cornwall, St Paulinus (Paul Aurelian).
38. Budock and Budock Vean, near Falmouth, Cornwall. St Budock.

3. The Saints of south-west England and their places of veneration.

ST ARILDA, 6-7c., martyr at Kington-by-Thornbury in Avon. The church at Oldbury-on-Severn is dedicated to her; 20th July.

ST ATHWENNA, 6c., Welsh (or Irish) saint. Advent in Cornwall.

ST BONIFACE of Crediton, 754, archbishop and martyr. A West Saxon of Crediton in Devon who became a missionary in Germany and Holland. He was elected archbishop of Mainz but suffered martyrdom at Dokkum trying to convert the heathen; 5th June.

ST BREACA (Brecha), 6c., Irish nun and follower of St Bridgit at Kildare in Ireland. She came to Cornwall and founded churches at Pencair, Trenwith and Talmeneth. The church at Breage in Cornwall is presumably dedicated to her; 27th October.

ST BREAGUE, 460. Irish saint and martyr at Hayle in Cornwall. He has sometimes been confused with St Breaca above; 4th June.

ST BREWARD (Branwaladr), 6c., Welsh monk. St Breward in Cornwall; he became first bishop of St Brelade (which is named after him) in Jeresy; 19th January or 9th February.

ST BURYAN (Boriana), 5c., Irish princess; a convert of St Patrick and founder of the church of St Buryan in Cornwall; 29th May.

ST CERRIAN (Keriane), 6c., Irish abbot. Egloskerry in Cornwall.

ST COLUMBA, 6c. Martyr at Ruthvoes in Cornwall. The church at St Columb Major in Cornwall is dedicated to her. 23rd October.

ST CONGAR, 6c., disciple of St Cadoc at Lanivet

in Cornwall. He also built some churches in Brittany; 13th February or 12th May.

ST CONSTANTINE, 575, Cornish prince and monk; disciple of St Petroc. Constantine near Padstow and Constantine near Helford. Other dedications at Dunsford and Milton Abbot, Devon. 9th March.

ST CREDAN, 6c., Irish monk, son of St Illogan and nephew of St Stediana. Sancreed church in Cornwall bears his name; 11th May.

ST CREWENNA, 5-6c., follower of St Breaca; Crowan in Cornwall.

ST CRIDA (Creda), 7c., Irish saint who came to Cornwall. The village of Creed near Tregony is named after her; 30th November.

ST CULBONE, 6c., Welsh monk and missionary. Culbone in Somerset.

ST DAY (Thei), Breton or Welsh abbot. St Day in Cornwall.

ST DOMINICA (Drusa), 700, Irish saint and sister of St Indract; martyr at Shapwick near Glastonbury in Somerset. The church at St Dominick in Cornwall is apparently named after her; 8th May.

ST ENODER, 6c., Welsh saint; husband of St Gwenappa and also uncle of St Gwynnog. St Enoder near Newquay in Cornwall.

ST ENODOC, 6c., Welsh Saint. St Enodoc in Cornwall.

ST ERME (Hermes), 3c., martyr. St Erme and Marazion, Cornwall.

ST ERTH (Ercus), 512, bishop of Slane in Ireland and brother of SS Ia and Euny. St Erth in Cornwall; 31st October.

ST EUNY (Uny), 530, Irish bishop in Cornwall. Capel Euny near Sancreed, and Marooney near Helston are both named after this saint. He is patron saint of a church near Lelant; 1st February.

ST EVAL (Uvelos), 6c., Welsh monk and son (or brother) of St Cenydd. St Eval near Padstow in Cornwall is his foundation.

ST GENNY (Genesius), 3c., Roman martyr. St Gennys in Cornwall.
ST GERAINT (Gerrenius), 522, King of Cornwall and father of St Justin. Polgerran and St-Gerans-in-Roseland could possibly be derived from his name, or another Cornish king Geraint. 16th May.
ST GERMOE, 5-6c., Irish king and bishop who came to Cornwall. The church at Germoe in Cornwall is dedicated to him. 30th July.
ST GONAND (Gonandas), 6c., hermit and disciple of St Breock at Pencarrow in Cornwall. Roche church is dedicated to him.
ST GORRAN (Guron or Wyron), 530, hermit at Bodmin, and Gorran in Cornwall; often associated with St Petroc; 7th April.
ST GULVAL (Gudwall), 6c., abbot of Locoal in Brittany. A church at Gulval in Cornwall is probably dedicated to him; 6th June.
ST GWENAPPA (Wynup), 6c., wife of St Enoder. Gwennap in Cornwall.
ST GWINEAR (Fingar), 480, Irish (or Welsh) monk and martyr at Hayle in Cornwall. Gwinear near Hayle bears his name; 23rd March.
ST GWITHIAN (Gothian), 6c., martyr at Riviere in Cornwall. His church at Gwithian stands amid the sand dunes; 1st November.

ST HYDROC, 6c., Welsh hermit at Lanhydroc, Cornwall; 5th May.

ST IA, 500. She sailed from Ireland to Cornwall on a large leaf; martyr at Plouye in Brittany. St Ives near Lelant; 3rd February.
ST ILLOGAN, 5-6c. Irish saint, son of king

Cormac and father of St Credan. Illogan near Redruth in Cornwall; 30th October.
ST INDRACT (Indractus), 700, Irish prince and martyr at Shapwick near Glastonbury; honoured at Glastonbury too; 8th May.
ST IVE (Ivy), 6c., Irish or Breton saint; St Ives in Cornwall.

ST JUDWARE (Judith or Aude), 7c., sister of St Sidwell and martyr at Halstock (Judith Hill) in Devon; 28th November.
ST JUST (Jestin), 550, hermit and son of Geraint king of Cornwall. Churches at St Just-in-Roseland and Lafrowda bear his name. St Just-in-Penwith is named after St Patrick's disciple.

ST KEA, 6c., monk; Landkey in Devon, Kea in Cornwall; 5th November.

ST LADOCA, 5-6c., Irish saint and abbess; Ladock in Cornwall.
ST LEVAN (Selevan), 6c., Irish (or Cornish) saint; St Levan in Cornwall. He may be the same as St Selyf of Lansallos near Fowey.
ST LIDE (Helidius), 5c., Irish or Welsh bishop and hermit in the Scilly Isles, where St Helen's bears his name; 8th August.
ST LIDGEAN, 7c., Irish abbot; Ludwan in Cornwall. 27th January.

ST MADRON (Madern), 6c., hermit at Madron in Cornwall; 17th May.
ST MANACA, 6c., Irish abbess; Manaccan in Cornwall; 14th October.
ST MANACCUS, 6c., bishop; Lanreath in Cornwall; 3rd August.
ST MAWES (Maudet) 6c., Irish monk; bishop in Brittany. A church at St Mawes in Cornwall is

ST GERMOE
from fresco in S Breague (restored).

ST MAWES
from statue at Ergué-Gaberic.

dedicated to him. 18th November.

ST MAWNAN, 7c., Irish bishop. Mawnan in Cornwall. 18th December.

ST MEUBRED (Mybard), 5c., Irish prince who came to Cornwall and became a hermit. The church at Cardingham in Cornwall bears his name.

ST MYLOR (Melar), 5-6c? Breton prince and martyr. The church at Mylor in Cornwall is dedicated to him. There are two more dedications at Linkinhorne, Cornwall, and Amesbury, Wiltshire. 1st October.

ST NEOT, 877, monk of Glastonbury and hermit at Bodmin. The church of St Neot in Cornwall venerates him. 31st July.

ST NEWLYN (Newlina or Noyale), 6c., martyr. Irish saint who settled in Cornwall, where St Newlyn's bears her name. She was later martyred at St Noyale in Brittany. 6th July.

ST PIALA, 5c., sister of St Gwinear; Phillack in Cornwall.

ST PINNOCK (Pynocus), 6c., Welsh saint. St Pinnock in Cornwall.

ST PIRAN (Perran), 5-6c., Irish or Welsh monk who founded the churches of Perranporth and Perranzubloe in Cornwall. He was regarded as the patron saint of Cornish tin miners. 5th March.

ST RAYNE (Reine), 3c? virgin and martyr. St Rayne's hill near Crewkerne in Somerset. She could be the French martyr of Alise.

ST RUAN (Rumon), 6c., Irish bishop who built churches at Ruan Major and Ruan Lanihorne in Cornwall. He was also honoured at Romansleigh and Tavistock in Devon. 30th August.

ST SELYF (Selevan), 6c., king of Cornwall and husband of St Wenn (Gwen) the sister of St Non. Lansallos near Fowey. 14th October.
ST SENNAIRA (Senara), 5-6c., Irish saint; Zennor in Cornwall.
ST SENNANAE, 5-6c., Irish female saint? Sennen in Cornwall.
ST SIDWELL, 700, virgin and martyr. The sister of SS Judware and Wulvella, she was murdered by pagans near Exeter in Devon. A church at Exeter is still dedicated to her. Sidwell is titular patron saint (with Wulvella) of Laneast in Cornwall. 31st July.
ST SITHNEY, 6c., Irish monk who became abbot of a monastery at Ploesezney (Guisseny) in Brittany. Sithney in Cornwall. 4th August.
ST STEDIANA, 6c., Irish saint. Stithians in Cornwall. 6th July.
ST SYMPHORIAN, 2c., Roman martyr at Autun in France. The church at Veryan in Cornwall is dedicated to him. 22nd August.

ST TEATH (Tetha), 570, is perhaps St Ita an Irish nun and follower of St Bridgit. St teath near Camelford in Cornwall. 15th January.
ST TORNEY (Tigernach), 549, Irish bishop and missionary in Cornwall. North Hill church is dedicated to him. 4th April.

ST URITH (Hieritha), 700, martyr at Chittlehampton in Devon. The churches at East Stowford in Devon, and at Nettlecombe in Somerset are dedicated to her. 8th July.

ST VEEP, 6c., is perhaps also St Gwenappa. St Veep in Cornwall.

ST WENDRON (Gwendron), 6c., mother of the

ST WINWALOE (GUENOLE)
from statue at Kernuz, Pont l'Abbe.

Irish St Lidgean (of Ludwan) in Cornwall. Wendron and Trelill in Cornwall.

ST WETHENOC, 6c., bishop, and brother of St Winwaloe. Towednack and possibly Landewednack (with St Winwaloe) in Cornwall.

ST WHYTE (Candida), 7c., Welsh or more likely a Saxon woman who was martyred by pagans at Charmouth in Dorset, after which her body was taken to Whitchurch Canonicorum church where her stone shrine can still be seen. 1st June.

ST WINWALOE (Winnol), 529, son of St Gwen Teibrian. He founded the monastery of Landevennec in Brittany, though he has church dedications at Gunwalloe and Lewannick in Cornwall. 3rd March.

ST WULFRIC, 1154, hermit; Haselbury in Somerset; 20th February.

ST WYLLOW, 5-6c., martyr; Lanteglos near Fowey in Cornwall.

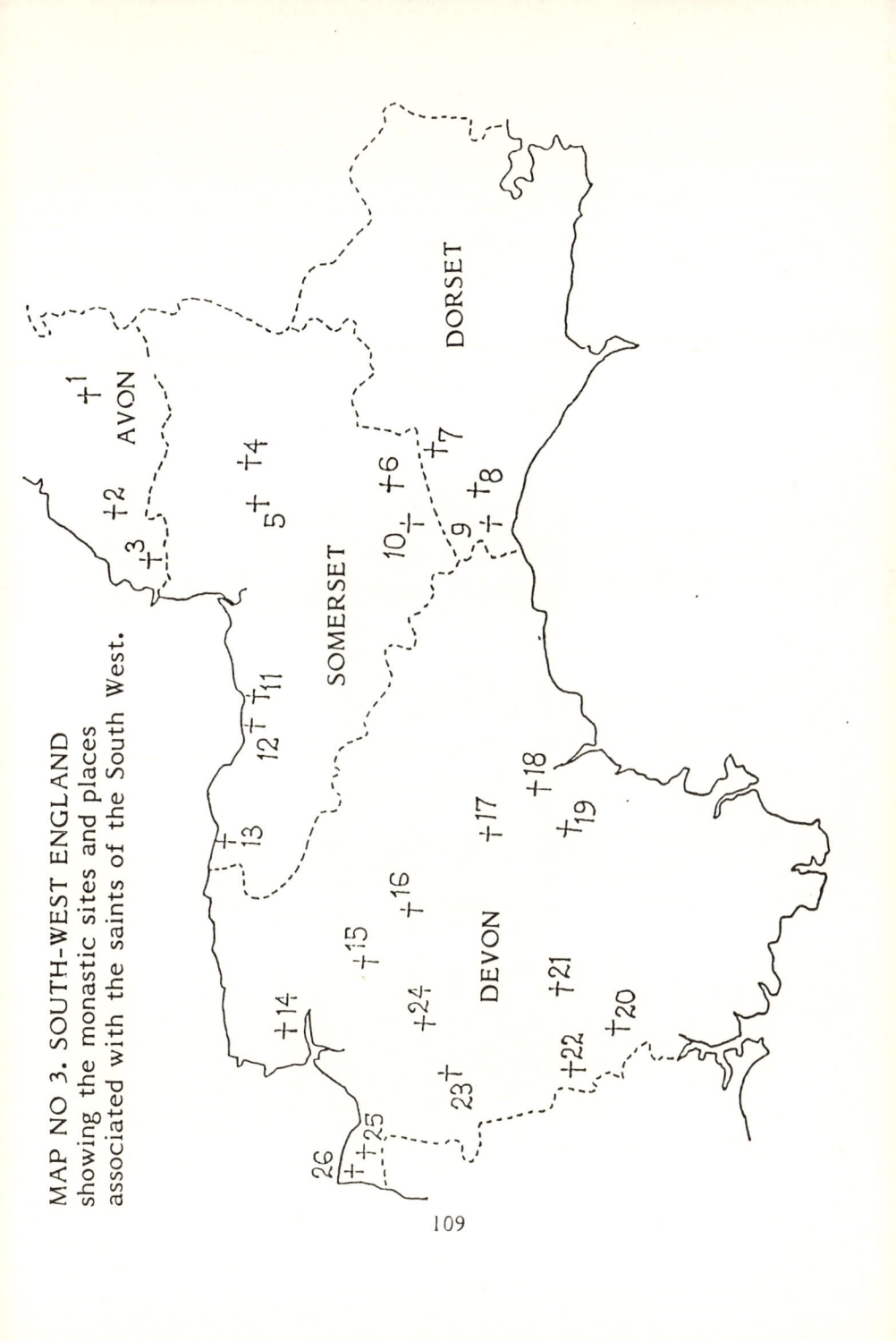

MAP NO 3. SOUTH-WEST ENGLAND
showing the monastic sites and places associated with the saints of the South West.

KEY TO MAP NO 3. SOUTH WEST ENGLAND: THE MONASTIC SITES AND PLACES associated with the saints of the South-West.

1. Keynsham, Avon,   St Keyne (or Kaegin)
2. Congresbury, Avon,   St Congar (Cungar).
3. Banwell, Nr. Weston-Super-Mare, Avon,
   St Congar (Cungar).
4. Glastonbury, Somerset,   SS David/Indract and others.
5. Shapwick, near Glastonbury, Somerset,
   SS Indract/Dominica.
6. Hazelbury Plucknett, Somerest,   St Wulfric (Ulfric).
7. Halstock, south of Yeovil, Dorset,   St Judware (Juditha).
8. Whitchurch Canonicorum, Dorset,   St Whyte (Candida).
9. Charmouth, near Lyme Regis, Dorset, St Whyte (Candida).
10. St Raine's Hill, Nr. Crewkerne, Somerest,
    St Raine (Reine).
11. Watchet, Somerset,   St Decuman.
12. Carhampton, Somerset,   St Caranoc (Carantocus).
13. Culbone, west of Porlock, Somerset,
    St Culbone.
14. Braunton, near Barnstaple, Devon, St Brannoc (or Brynach).
15. Chittlehampton, Somerset, St Urith (Hierytha).
16. Romansleigh, near South Molton, Devon,
    St Rumon (Ruan).
17. Crediton, Devon,   St Boniface of Crediton*.
18. Exeter, Devon,   St Sidwell.

*Doubt has been cast on Crediton as the birthplace of St Boniface; see e.g. King, R.J. Proc. Somerset Archaeological Society, xx, 1874.

19. Dunsford, west of Exeter, Devon,
                              St Constantine.
20. Tavistock, Devon,   St Rumon (Ruan).
21. Lydford, near Bridestow, Devon,   St Petroc.
22. Bradstone, near Launceston, Devon,   St Non
                              (Nonnita).
23. Holsworthy, Devon,   St Petroc.
24. Newton St Petroc, Devon, St Petroc.
25. Philham, near Hartland, Devon,   St Cleer
                              (Clether, Clarus).
26. Stoke and Hartland, north Devon,   St Nectan
                              (Nighton).

BIBLIOGRAPHY

Barber, Chris, **Mysterious Wales** (David & Charles, Newton Abbot, 1982; Paladin paperback, 1983).

Barber, Chris, **More Mysterious Wales** (David & Charles, Newton Abbot, 1986; Paladin paperback, 1987).

Baring-Gould, S. and Fisher, J. **The Lives of the British Saints** (4 vols., London, 1907-13).

Bord, Janet and Colin, **Sacred Waters** (Granada, 1985; Paladin paperback 1986).

Bowen, E. G. **The Settlements of the Celtic Saints in Wales** (University of Wales Press, Cardiff, 1956).

Doble, G. H. **The Saints of Cornwall**, Part 1 (1960).

Hencken, E. R. **Traditions of the Welsh Saints** (D. S. Brewer, 1987).

Sian Victory, **The Celtic Church in Wales** (SPCK 1977).

Also published by
LLANERCH:

LIVES OF THE
BRITISH SAINTS
by Baring-Gould & Fisher

THE LIFE OF ST COLUMBA
by Adamnan

SYMBOLISM OF THE
CELTIC CROSS
by Derek Bryce

TRADITIONS AND HEARTHSIDE STORIES
OF WEST CORNWALL
by W. Bottrell

POPULAR ROMANCES OF THE
WEST OF ENGLAND: THE TRADITIONS
OF OLD CORNWALL
by J. Hunt

From booksellers. For
a complete list, write to
LLANERCH PUBLISHERS
FELINFACH, LAMPETER,
DYFED. SA48 8PJ.